American
Wines
and
Wine
Cooking

American Wines and Wine Cooking

**Shirley Sarvis
and
Robert Thompson**

Photography by Arie deZanger
Drawings by Jean Simpson

 CREATIVE HOME LIBRARY®
In Association with Better Homes and Gardens®
Meredith Corporation

CHL CREATIVE HOME LIBRARY®

Library of Congress Cataloging in Publication Data

Sarvis, Shirley.
American wines and wine cooking.
1. Wine and wine making—United States. 2. Cookery
(Wine) I. Thompson, Robert, 1934- joint author.
II. Title.
TP557.S25   641.2′2′0973   73-15564

ISBN 0-696-24700-3

Art direction and design by
A.J. Pollicino

Photographs by
Arie deZanger: cover and pp. ii, 9, 45, 63, 105, 121, 149, 165, 177
Robert Thompson: pp. vi, viii

Table linens courtesy of Vera, Inc.
China and kitchen utensils courtesy of Hammacher Schlemmer
Glassware courtesy of Minners & Co., Inc.
Kitchen appliances for food preparation courtesy of Frigidaire
Phonetic pronunciations courtesy of Continental Translation Service, Inc.

iv

About the Authors

Shirley Sarvis has been a writer and consultant on foods and wines for more than a decade. She is the author or co-author of eight published cookbooks—including *Table for Two, A Taste of Portugal,* and *San Francisco Firehouse Favorites*—and innumerable magazine articles. A resident of San Francisco, she travels abroad frequently to test and taste fine foods and wines the world over.

v

Robert Thompson is also a San Franciscan and a veteran reporter of the American wine scene. His weekly column on wine appears regularly in the *San Francisco Examiner,* and he has been a frequent writer and consultant for The Wine Institute.

vi

Contents

Introduction

Americans knew about wine a long time ago. After all, it was Benjamin Franklin who said that wine is constant proof that God loves us and loves to see us happy, and it was George Washington who served mutton and Madeira to guests at Mount Vernon.

But we lost our familiarity with wine during Prohibition. That era obscured the fact that good wine civilizes the people who drink it. It also laid waste to thousands of acres of our best vineyards.

During the early 1960s, the American public began to get properly reacquainted with the diversity of wine as a beverage and its complexity as a hobby. It was then, as knowledgeable wine drinkers discovered, that both good and great American wines were becoming available in reasonable quantities.

Happily, it was not only Americans who started boosting their home-grown product in the early 1960s. The English, having no vineyards to speak of in their own country, long have ruled as impartial arbiters in the world of wine. And English connoisseurs began to take a positive interest in American wines, especially the ones from California, at the same time the American public did.

The absence of large amounts of fine American wines until recent years owes itself to the fact that it took several decades to restore all the great pre-Prohibition vineyards. The old saw about the best wines coming from a small area of the hill may exaggerate a bit, but there is more than a germ of truth in it. Wine grapes are uncannily fussy about their surroundings, and no wine is better than the grapes that go into it. It is only with the 1970s that we are drinking enough wine to justify big new plantings of fine grapes in fine districts.

If we have reasonable assurances that American wine is well worth the drinking, we do not have reasonable assurances that it is an easy subject to master. Wine is infinitely complex, well worth the devotion that hobbyists bring to it.

However, there is a free choice between taking up wine as a hobby and taking it up as a refreshing glass. At one point or another, some of us inhale deeply from a glass of wine and begin to smell a whole garden—sun, soil, leaf, flower, and fruit. Those who do are likely to find themselves increasingly drawn to wine as a hobby. The rest of us will inhale and sniff a glass of good wine, but no more; these are the casual drinkers who take great pleasure from wine but only a few pains with it.

For all of us, drinking American wines is an excellent way to begin exploring the world of wine. We should not stop within our borders, but we can learn both beginning and advanced lessons about wine from our own bottlings for two sound reasons.

First, American wines are good.

Second, the geography of vineyards in America can be learned more quickly than that of most other countries. The place names are relatively few and relatively familiar.

The following pages provide a solid framework for thinking about which wines to use when, what to drink wine with, and how to cook with wine. Everything else you need to know is in the glass.

1

Getting Acquainted with American Wine

In Georges Simenon's mystery stories, Chief Inspector Maigret frequently goes into a café and asks for "a white wine, please." An intelligent American reading the passage believes that Maigret gets what he wants, but when the same American goes into a restaurant, he too often thinks *he* cannot order wine unless he knows the name of the producer, the name of the vineyard, the vintage year, and a raft of other information.

We Americans are just beginning to learn what the French knew in 1776—that wine is democratic enough to satisfy the person who wants only a drink, as well as the hobbyist who insists on having an immortal experience each time he raises a glass. A Frenchman also has the advantage of being able to order an ordinary wine that has no designation other than "white," while we tend to burden the most routine of our wines with the name of the producer and some name that seems more specific than just white or red.

Indeed, because wine has been made in thousands of places from hundreds of grape varieties for thousands of years, it has a multitude of names—all authentic. Nevertheless, there are five general names, or classes, that cover the entire field: red wine, white wine, sparkling wine, appetizer wine, and dessert wine. All other names are elaborations, in the same way Mustang is an elaboration on Ford, and Ford, an elaboration on automobile.

The first step toward getting wine comfortably integrated into one's life is to drink ordinary wine with ordinary meals. People just becoming acquainted with wine are well advised to buy two cases of unpretentious, medium-priced table wine—one red, one white—and to drink these fairly regularly with everyday dinners. After this experience, a newcomer has a secure standard for judging other wine candidates for his daily table as better or worse, worth the price he paid or not.

Sparkling, appetizer, and dessert wines are somewhat special cases. The range of choice is much smaller, for they are used less often and they do not have to go well with a whole dinner. In other words, there is less need to fret over them.

Reading Labels

Wine labels explain a great deal about what the bottle contains. By law, all the following information must appear on the label.

Name of the producer   As with any brand name, the signature of those responsible for the product hints at the style of the product. If you like one wine from a producer, you are likely to find his others enjoyable.

Vintage date or year   The naming of a particular year on a label means that the wine is from 95 to 100 percent made from grapes harvested during that year. The information is useful because it indicates the age of the wine and, to serious hobbyists, is a key to the subtle differences between one year's grapes and another's.

Only a small percentage of the world's wines carries a vintage date. The omission of the vintage date is, in effect, an invitation to drink the wine as soon as it is bought. Either the wine is of a type that suits itself to immediate consumption or it is a blend of several vintages already matured.

Geographical origin   The label must state where the wine's grapes were grown. A label that reads "American" simply means that the grapes were grown on this continent. Many East Coast wines are so labeled because they have substantial amounts of California wine blended in to temper the flavor of the native grapes.

If the label names a state (California, Ohio, Washington, etc.), 100 percent of the grapes in the wine must have come from vineyards in that state. The exception is New York, which requires only 75 percent of the grapes in its wines to be native.

2

The label may also name a specific region within a state, such as Finger Lakes, Napa Valley, Sonoma, or Santa Clara. A label that also has a vintage date ensures that 100 percent of the grapes were grown within the region named. If there is no vintage date, the percentage may range from 75 to 100 percent, with the rest of the grapes coming from within the state.

Name of wine   Wines bear varietal, generic, or proprietary names.

VARIETALS are named after a grape variety (Pinot Noir [Peeno Nwar], Grenache [Grehnash], Niagara, and so forth). At least 51 percent of any American wine so named must be from the namesake grape. In practice the percentage usually runs between 75 and 100.

GENERICS made in the United States are named mostly for European regions, such as Rhine, Burgundy, and Chianti (Kee-an-tee). There are no requirements on the grape varieties used to make our generic wines, nor are the wines required to adhere to narrow limits of style. As a result, some bear a considerable resemblance to their original inspirations, but most stray wide from the mark.

PROPRIETARIES are a subdivision of the generics. Instead of calling a wine Rhine, a producer will name it Rhineskeller, Rhine Castle, or some other coinage that he registers as an exclusive trademark. The proprietor may use any blend of grape varieties he wishes.

Alcohol content   If the figure on the label for alcohol content reads from 10½ to 13½, the wine in the bottle is either table or sparkling wine, the result of a natural fermentation of grapes. If the figure reads from 17 to 19½, the wine in the bottle is either appetizer or dessert wine, its alcohol level having been raised by the addition of grape brandy. If the figures are either less than 10½ or around 14, chances are that the liquid within is a mixture of wine and other natural flavoring agents, as described on page 5.

Produced and bottled by_____. This statement means that 51 percent or more of the wine in the bottle was made and aged by the company named on the label.

Made and bottled by_____ .   This means that as little as 10 percent or as much as 50 percent of the wine in the bottle was made and aged by the company named on the label. The remainder was bought by the bottler from another wine maker.

Perfected and bottled by _____.   This and all other expressions of the sort indicate that the bottler aged wine that was fermented by somebody else. This is not as unimportant as it sounds. The length of aging, the blending, and other techniques have a great deal to do with the way a wine tastes in the end.

Bottled by_____.   This means only that the company named on the label bottled the wine.

The city named on a label as the site of the company may or may not be the location of the company's wine cellars; some wineries list only the location of their business offices on the label.

Sparkling Wine Labels

Wines with bubbles carry some separate label information about the way in which the bubbles got there.

If the label says the wine is champagne (or sparkling Burgundy), the bubbles are a result of the wine's having been naturally fermented in a closed container. There are three basic methods for making champagne, each of which is described below. The label will indicate which was used to make the particular bottle.

If the label (usually the neck label) says "fermented in this bottle," the wine was made sparkling in the traditional French *méthode champenoise* by

3

conducting a second fermentation within the same bottle you hold. The process is slow and expensive.

If the label says only "bottle fermented," the wine was made sparkling by conducting a second fermentation in a bottle but in a different bottle from the one you hold. An efficient technique, called either the "transfer process" or the "Carstens process," simplifies the problem of getting the yeasts and other sediments out of the bottle after the fermentation is complete.

If the label says "bulk process" or "Charmat process," the wine was made sparkling in a large sealed tank and then bottled under pressure so that the bubbles could not escape. This is quick and far less expensive than either of the first two methods.

If a bubbly wine's label says "crackling," the wine may not be called champagne. It has fewer bubbles than sparkling wine, and it is developed through a fermentation technique slightly different from any of the above.

If the label says "carbonated," the bubbles are a result not of fermentation but of carbon dioxide having been pumped into the wine in the same way it is pumped into soda pop. Such a wine cannot be called champagne or even sparkling.

Flavored Wine Labels

Recently, a great market has developed for wines known as "Special Natural Flavored." The legal descriptive term tells the whole story. These beverages use natural flavors in company with rather neutral wines; in effect, they are premixed punches, or coolers. Specific examples include Dubonnet, Key Largo, and Spañada.

The key to knowing what is in the bottle is in the small type at the bottom of the label, where the nongrape ingredients must be listed.

Talking about Wine

Once upon a time, King Edward VII of England said that first you look at a wine, then smell it, then sip it, and then, sirrahs, you talk about it. Talking is easy for kings; the audience must listen. Even so, old Edward had a point. Talk helps to sort out the complex impressions a good wine makes on its imbiber.

Talk can go too far. The ethereal rambles of some connoisseurs, or would-be connoisseurs, have served too many times to intimidate newcomers to the world of wine.

To avoid this, remember that there are only four true tastes—sweet, sour, salt, and bitter. With food and wine alike, all else is *smell,* and smell is what you remember from your experience. If you say, "Ah, this wine reminds me of a whole field full of flowers on a spring morning," and somebody else wants to disagree, all you have to do is turn the discussion to your particular field of flowers, and the other fellow will be hard pressed to win.

A second point to remember is that the words *dry, sweet, tart, flat, thin, full-bodied, young,* and *old*—plus a few logical synonyms—provide enough vocabulary to get anybody through a discussion of any wine fit to drink.

Dry and *sweet* are opposites and are basic qualities in all wines. *Dry* means that all the grape sugar was fermented into alcohol when the wine was made. A dry wine tastes dry. *Off-dry* and *medium-dry* are useful for describing wines that are perceptibly sweet but decidedly not cloying. *Mellow* is a euphemism for "very sweet," sometimes found on the label of a table wine.

Tart and *flat* are another pair of straightforward, and basic, opposites. When a grape forms in the spring, it is all acid with no sugar. As the fruit ripens, its acid level declines and its sugar content rises. Exactly how the two balance when the grape is picked does much to govern a wine's tartness or flabbiness (flatness). Everybody who has tasted grapefruit juice knows what tart is. Flabby wines, on the other hand, leave the same sort of impression that soda pop does after the bubbles have disappeared.

Thin is at the other end of the pole from *full-bodied.* These words deal with the "feel" of a wine in your mouth. A thin wine goes down like water, leaving no memories; a full-bodied wine lingers in the mouth. Substance is more complicated to describe than sweet or tart, but not much. A wine that is full-bodied and flabby can be called "fat," while one that is full-bodied and tart deserves an adjective that suggests some muscle—*robust* is the usual standby we use.

Aroma (young) and *bouquet* (old) are the last pair of opposites, but being smells, they are elusive and abstract. *Aroma* is the smell of the grape preserved in the wine; *bouquet* is the smell that develops during and after fermentation. As a wine ages, its aroma grows ever fainter while its bouquet becomes more and more pronounced. Thus, aroma correlates with young wine and bouquet with old.

Aroma encompasses that all-purpose catchword *fruity,* as well as the wine snob's ultimate weapon, *varietal characteristic*—which is to say that the wine smells like the variety of grape from which it was made. A wine is young, or fruity, when it reminds you of fresh fruit flavors, usually berries or a tree fruit.

A wine is bouquetish when its smell reminds you of almost anything other than fruit. This could be a spice, a cedar forest, or a cigar. In reality the bouquet is made up of alcohol, yeasts, oxidation, and—sometimes—the wood smell from barrels.

5

A poet can spend a lifetime expanding the basic wine vocabulary. For example, instead of admitting that a wine is thin, sharp, and lacking in fruit, snobs will say that it is spinsterish or miserly.

Incidentally, a really fine wine does not evoke any of these extreme descriptions. An outstanding bottle will be perfectly balanced between dry and sweet, tart and flabby, thin and fat, young-fruity and old-bouqueted. You will know one when you come to it.

Dessert wines are, of course, an exception to this in dryness or sweetness, but the great ones never cloy no matter how much sugar is in them.

Getting Down to Choices

It has been assumed in this country that people who know a lot about wine must have different kinds of taste buds than other people and that they experience a whole different set of sensations when they drink. Not so. We have, most of us, about the same physical equipment; that is, we taste sweet at about the same concentrations, and likewise bitter.

Most of us sense about the same number of aromas, too—several thousand on the average, which makes us very sensitive, indeed. For example, there is scholarly research proving that almost everybody prefers tomato juice packaged in a tin-plated can to the same juice from a glass jar. We do not have to see the can to know the difference, for tin imparts a faint but unmistakable nuance to the juice flavor. Habit has made having that nuance important.

The subtleties of wine are similarly easy or even easier to spot.

Individually, of course, we enjoy having differing tolerances for the things we taste and smell. Any two of us may begin to perceive bitter at the same concentration, but one of us will like the taste of it more than the other does. Experience will not change our minds very much about these fundamental likes and dislikes. The only difference between a wine devotee and a casual drinker is that the former has learned precise standards for many wines and can admire superior quality even when he does not like the taste of it.

There are three fundamental qualities to want or not to want in a wine each time you sit down to drink one: sweet or a lack of it; sharpness or a lack of it; and intense flavor or a lack of it. There is nothing unique in this; it is true of all food and drink. Wine merely allows subtler, more satisfying choices to be made than most foods.

The following chapters on specific wines conform to this basic line of thought. In them, we tell not what we think you should like but rather how to look for something you probably will like.

Later on, in the recipe chapters, we do recommend the wines that we prefer—first in the most general terms possible, then in the most specific. If you agree with us, fine; if you do not, you should be able to figure out in what way we differ and to make your own choices.

Wines in General

Although wine does reduce to its five classes, one can experience vast enjoyment in the details of variance within the classes. Otherwise, poets would not write about wine and people would not collect it by the thousands of bottles. For the hobbyist who wants to know everything, wine provides a lifetime of extraordinarily pleasing learning experiences, with almost no repetition. The man who wants to know much less still owes it to his taste buds to look beyond the color of the wine in its bottle.

The important differences between one bottle of wine and another are caused by the following factors: the specific kind of grapes used to make a wine; the place that those grapes grew; and the attitudes of the man who fermented the grapes into wine.

The first vital detail is that California has a tradition of wine making separate from that of the rest of the country. Since the mid-1880s, California has used the same species and varieties of grapes as are used in the great wines of Europe. The species is *Vitis vinifera*. The varieties within the species number into the thousands, although only about 100 of them are used to make most California wine. The most prestigious of them lend their names to the **varietal wines: Cabernet Sauvignon (Kabernay So-vee-gnon), Pinot Noir, Pinot Blanc (Peeno Blan), Chardonnay (Shar-do-nay), and Johannisberg Riesling (Rees-ling),** to name a few.

The rest of the country—including such widely separated regions as New York, Ohio, and Washington State—traditionally has used several native species of grapes, especially *Vitis labrusca*. The best-known grape of the labrusca species is the Concord; other native varieties include Catawba, Delaware, and Niagara. Increasingly, states other than California are leaning toward French-American hybrid grapes—American native grapes that have been crossed with the European viniferas. Baco Noir is one example of this. And where climate permits, there are tentative plantings of *Vitis viniferas*.

Generally, wines from viniferas have subtle, complex flavors whereas those from native grapes have strong, forthright tastes. People who are completely accustomed to vinifera flavors usually find the native wines strange and not always likeable; the reverse is just as likely.

Within species, individual grape varieties have distinctive flavors. These flavors can be captured in wine as long as the varieties are kept separate. This is the essence of varietal wine.

Generic wines, made from blends of several grape varieties, have less identifiable flavors. Comparisons are not easy to make, but a blackberry, loganberry, or raspberry jelly each would be a varietal, while one mixture of the three would produce a generic "berry" jelly. Just as generic berry jelly can be very good, so can generic wines.

In California, varietals tend to be expensive, and they tend to come from the coastal vineyards that range north and south of San Francisco Bay. Most of the generics come from vineyards in the Great Central Valley and do not cost as much. However, there are coastal generics and valley varietals with prices in the middle range.

Varietal wines tend to be reserved for special occasions while the generics do daily duty at ordinary dinners (Chardonnay with lobster; Chablis [Sha-blee] with tuna-noodle casserole). But there are many exceptions. If there is a rule of thumb, it is to pair an expensive wine with an elegant meal and to drink less expensive ones for everyday.

Of the five basic classes of wine, only the reds and whites (plus rosé) are wines in more or less natural form. Ferment ripe red grapes with a minimum of human intervention, and the result will be red wine. Take care to separate the skins and seeds of either red or green grapes from the juice before fermenting, and the result will be white wine. (Separate juice from red skins after a few hours instead of several days, and the result is rosé wine.)

The other classes of wine require more extensive preparation.

To get sparkling wine, a wine maker must first make wine in the regular way. Then he must add tiny amounts of sugar and yeast to that wine, which is in a closed container, setting off a secondary fermentation. Having a closed container prevents the carbon dioxide of fermentation from escaping, thus forming the fine festive bubbles.

To produce sherry, the wine maker must expose white wine to air or to heat so that it turns brown and acquires the characteristic flavor. To get dessert wine, he must add grape brandy to augment the alcohol.

The following chapters sort out American wines one class at a time.

Sherry-broiled Shrimp, p. 73

2

The Red Wines of America

A wine judge, pressed for his choice of the world's greatest wine, would undoubtedly name a red. A laboring man, asked for his choice of a dinner wine at the end of a day in the fields, would be just as likely to name a red.

For the wine judge, great red wines offer the most satisfying tests of his palate. For the worker, a young red wine has enough strength to go with the food he wants for his well-earned dinner.

There is room for such differing kinds of enthusiasm because there is literally more to like about a red wine. Because the juice of the grapes is fermented in contact with the seeds and skins, a red wine has strengths not found in white, rosé, and sparkling wines.

While white wines refresh with cool, light flavors, red wines reawaken the palate with sharp, aggressive tastes of their own. Hence, red wines usually are sought as companions to rich meats like lamb and beef and also to rich or spicy sauces.

Most red wines are meant to be drunk soon after they are bought, while they have the brisk charms of youth. A few vintage-dated varietals, however, have the capacity to age for year after year. These wines gain in complexity as they grow smoother. Few of them are completely agreeable at the beginnings of their careers, but when they finally get where they are going, they prove the wisdom of waiting.

There are three essential choices among red wines: fruity, mellow (which is to say sweet), and full-dry.

Fruity Reds

GENERICS—California Burgundy and claret; native American
　　　Burgundy and claret
VARIETALS—Gamay, Gamay Beaujolais (Gamah Bo-zho-lay),
　　　Gamay Noir, Grignolino, Pinot St. George, Zinfandel; from
　　　French-American hybrids: Baco Noir, Chelois

Because the fruity reds tend to be the most delicately flavored of red wines, they are the most versatile companions to food. For the same reason, they are highly adaptable as cooking ingredients.

Inexpensive wines in this category tend to be slightly sweeter than the more expensive bottlings.

All these wines, with the possible exception of expensive Zinfandels, are intended to be bought for immediate use.

11

California Burgundy

As a name, California Burgundy describes a vast amount of wine. Most of it is just inexpensive red wine, a counterpart to the kind that goes—without a name—onto family dinner tables in Europe. Such inexpensive American wines are nearly always sound because they come from well-equipped, competently staffed, stable businesses. This does not mean that you will like all California Burgundies equally, but if you dislike one, your distaste will stem from the style of the wine, not from an excess of vinegar or some other spoilage.

Some California Burgundies are more distinctive and fairly expensive.

If you seek a soft red with an evident tinge of sweet, look first among the inexpensive Burgundies from California's Great Central Valley. The label will say only "California" as an appellation of origin, but the small type at the bottom will state that the wine was bottled in Lodi, Modesto, Fresno, Bakersfield, or one of the smaller communities nearby. If you want a drier, more tart wine, pay more money and experiment among the bottlings from wineries located in Sonoma, Napa, Santa Clara, San Benito, or Monterey, which are the coastal counties near San Francisco.

Mountain red is another way to say California Burgundy.

California Claret

Claret has nearly disappeared as a generic name on American wine labels. Where it does exist, there is no systematic way to distinguish it from Burgundy. If you find a claret you like, it is good red wine. If you don't like it, it is not so good. This is also the way to judge Burgundy.

Burgundies and clarets from states other than California will be marked by the flavors of native species of grapes rather than the vinifera species. Most of these wines are just a bit sweet.

Gamay, Gamay Beaujolais, Gamay Noir, and Pinot St. George

These reds are all varietals, and all are made from grape varieties that originated in the Burgundy region of France.

Honest tasters will admit that these wines are very hard to distinguish from one another in blind tastings, when the labels are hidden and only your tongue can guide you.

Each grape variety produces a lightly flavored, soft, agreeable wine that is best drunk young, when its fruity charms are at their peak. These wines have more definite character than does an average generic Burgundy and are priced accordingly.

A well-made Gamay serves well when a good cut of beef deserves a fairly special wine but when you do not wish to spend the money for a truly expensive bottle of red.

Grignolino

This Italian grape from the Piedmont area produces in California a tart, refreshing red wine of highly individual character. Some of its admirers say its flavor has almost a hint of oranges. In any case, it is a superlative accompaniment to lamb and a fine companion to spicy beef stews. Grignolino is hard to find, for only two or three wineries make it and all of them are small. Still, it is not very expensive and is worth seeking out as a distinctive dry red wine.

Zinfandel

This grape grows everywhere and produces many kinds of wine: cheap, expensive, red, rosé, even port. If at first you don't find Zinfandel agreeable, try again; you are bound to like one.

In the coastal counties of California—especially Napa and Sonoma—Zinfandel produces a light, often elegant red wine. Some of the best ones compete with good Cabernet Sauvignons. In the Great Central Valley, the grape produces a burlier wine, often softened with a bit of sweet. Whichever type you prefer, Zinfandel makes an extraordinarily reliable and interesting wine to have with a meal. The greatest compliment to it was paid by a wine maker who said that if he were forced to choose one wine to drink every day for the rest of his life, he would pick Zinfandel and be glad.

Baco Noir

This is the relatively new name for a relatively old French-American hybrid grape (formerly Baco No. 1) grown in the Atlantic seaboard states. It is also the name of a New York varietal wine of distinctive character. It is very tart wine, leaving an impression kindred to the kind you get from eating a slightly underripe blackberry; you wince, but you like it. Of all the wines made in America from grapes other than vinifera, this one finds the quickest favor with Europeans and European-oriented wine drinkers.

Chelois

Also made from a French-American hybrid grape, Chelois wine is more Yankee than Gallic in flavor and is more sweet than dry by nature.

13

Mellow Reds

GENERICS—Chianti, Vino da Tavola, Vino Pastoso, or any other
name that suggests Italian country wine
VARIETALS—Barberone; from native grapes; Concord.

Mellow, in the case of red wines, means rather sweet wine. These wines
border on being suitable as dessert wines, in lieu of port. (Every now and
again, a California coastal winery will make a fairly dry Chianti, but this is
rare.)

As mealtime wines, Chianti, Vino Pastoso, and other California reds
bearing Italian names all serve the same purposes. They are drunk to wash
down pizza, pasta, meat loaf, and other casual entrées. The intention is to
match the homemade red that enlivens Italian family dinner tables. The accent is on amiability more than finesse.

Almost none of these wines is made outside California, probably because most of America's wine makers of Italian descent settled in the conge-
nial Mediterranean climate of the West Coast.

The Concord grape, native to the East Coast and widely planted there,
produces a mellow red wine. The flavor is quite familiar to Americans—it
is the same as is found in grape juice, grape-ade, grape jelly, and other products in which this grape is used. Embody that flavor in sweet wine, and you
learn what Concord is all about. Especially when it is made in the kosher
style, Concord is taken as a convivial glass rather than a conscientious part
of dinner.

Full-Dry Reds

VARIETALS—Barbera, Cabernet Sauvignon, Petite Sirah, Pinot
Noir, and on rare occasions, Zinfandel

These are the wines that delight hobbyists because they can be stored in
wine cellars to age into elegant maturity, fit for serving on state occasions.

People who genuinely love wine choose favorites from among these
varietals, buy them in large quantities, and then drink them at any time during the aging process, taking pleasure not only from the taste of each bottle
but from the growth of the wine to its peak.

Reds of this quality have such forceful characters that they impose
themselves strongly on a meal. Beef and game are good with these wines,
both when the wines are young and forever after. As the wines gain subtlety

with age, wise drinkers think to pair them more often with lamb, sweet-breads, veal in brown sauces, and other more delicately flavored dishes.

It should be noted here that age in a wine is the most relative of its factors. All the wines in this section deserve four years of aging; from that point on, the length of time to age an individual wine will vary according to its particular strengths. Beyond four years, too, storage conditions exert a great influence.

Barbera

In some ways an enigma, this red is fuller and far more winy than any of the Gamays, but it does not develop the complex balance of flavors to be found in Cabernet Sauvignon or Pinot Noir. Barbera is a bold, rich, tannic wine eminently suited to game, spicy Mediterranean sauces, and plain meat. Its tannins pucker the drinker's mouth, making the wine seem quite dry. It does not need great age, but it does not suffer from it. In short this is a highly serviceable and attractive wine.

Cabernet Sauvignon

The Cabernet Sauvignon grape produces California's biggest, longest-lived red wine, just as it makes France's most age-worthy wine in the Médoc, near Bordeaux. A young wine from this grape can, if its maker wishes, be highly tannic and rough, but nobody offers it that way. Depending on personal conviction, wine makers either blend aged wines with young ones to achieve the softness that age brings or store vintage-dated wines long enough to smooth the sharp corners. These are the wines that will age fifteen years or more.

Cabernet Sauvignon has a distinctive flavor, less changeable from district to district than those of most other varietals. When expert tasters try to describe the taste, they usually compare it to teas or to herbs, a clear indication that its flavor is very sharp and very dry rather than round and fruity.

It is a wine to serve with first-rate meat for first-rate guests.

Petite Sirah

This red shares many characteristics with Barbera and complements the same array of foods with equal facility. Yet Petite Sirah tastes very much different from Barbera.

Some people prefer one to the other; some people like them about equally. In any case if you have ever wondered what varietal characteristics can mean, put a bottle of each on the table some night, try them side by side, and you will know.

Pinot Noir

This wine's reputation in California lags slightly behind that of Cabernet Sauvignon. From the classic grape of French Burgundy, Pinot Noir diverges widely from that model in California, being lighter and, in some ways, subtler. It ages almost as well as French Burgundy—up to eight years with ease and, on occasion, to infinity—but the overall character is specifically Californian.

Some people greatly prefer Pinot Noir, no matter what its reputation, to Cabernet Sauvignon because it is a rounder, less biting wine. To put it another way, the man who likes the last cup of Chinese tea—without any sugar—from the pot will be a Cabernet man, while the person who would rather have the first cup with sugar will favor Pinot Noir.

The foods to serve with Pinot Noir are the same ones that would be served with Cabernet.

Rosé Wines

GENERICS—Rosé, vin rosé, pink, pink Chablis
VARIETALS—Cabernet Rosé, Gamay Rosé, Grenache Rosé, Grignolino Rosé, Zinfandel Rosé; from native grapes: Catawba Rosé, Delaware Rosé

It is easy to say too little about rosés and hard to say too much. People who live where the summers are long and hot will find that rosés can be delightful.

In essence, a rosé is a red wine made to resemble as nearly as possible a white one. Grapes ordinarily used to make red wine are fermented and aged in the manner of white wine grapes. The result is a slightly more berryish wine than any white can be. A handful of rosés are dry; most are medium-dry; some are definitely sweet.

The natural foods for rosé wines are picnic hams and pork chops. But a barbecued steak on a sweltering summer night will taste much better with a cold rosé instead of a weighty, warmish red.

All the generic rosés tend to be sweet. Among California generics, bottlings from the north coast may be a tiny bit drier and more tart than those from the Central Valley. Generic rosés from New York and other Eastern wineries will be marked by the flavor of native grapes but otherwise will not differ vastly from California's. Pink Chablis differs from other rosés in having a trace of spritz (bubbles).

Among the varietals, Grenache Rosé has a perfumy character that accentuates sweet, fruity impressions. Gamay Rosé tends to be similar to Grenache, although the fruit flavors are more muted.

Cabernet, Grignolino, and Zinfandel rosés are likely to be the driest and most tart of the California rosés, the ones most likely to pass muster with confirmed red wine drinkers.

The Catawba grape produces a delicately flavored rosé with distinctly sweet overtones. Delaware grapes make a softer, fuller wine that is of the native type.

America's Red Wines

Generics

Barberone	Chianti	Mountain Red
Burgundy	Claret	Vino Rosso

Varietals

Barbera	Gamay Beaujolais	Pinot St. George
Cabernet	Grenache	(also known as Red Pinot)
Cabernet Sauvignon	Grignolino	Royalty
Charbono	Petite Sirah	Ruby Cabernet
Gamay	Pinot Noir	Zinfandel

Native or Hybrid Varietals

Baco Noir	Chelois	Concord

America's Rosé Wines

Generics

Pink Chablis	Rosé	Vin Rosé

Varietals

Cabernet Rosé	Grenache Rosé	Zinfandel Rosé
Gamay Rosé	Grignolino Rosé	

Native or Hybrid Varietals

Catawba	Isabella

3

The White Wines of America

White wines tend to resemble the soft, fresh flavors of fresh fruit. People getting acquainted with wine usually find these familiar tastes easier to like than the sharper flavors of red wine. Some wine snobs say whites are really not wine, but even the most dedicated of red wine makers have soft spots in their hearts for at least one white.

The old maxim about white wines being suited to seafood and poultry is useful because it matches delicately flavored foods with delicate wines. However, the range of food that white wines complement is broader than this. The lighter white wines also go well with light hors d'oeuvres and creamy casseroles, while the more flavorful whites can be drunk with fresh fruit, rich hors d'oeuvres, or alone as afternoon coolers.

White wines vary more noticeably than reds in their colors, in the intensity of their flavors, and in the range from dry to sweet. Flavor intensities derive mainly from the choice of grape varieties. Sweetness is controlled entirely by the wine maker. Color is a product of both forces. These variations mean that white wines are sometimes more difficult to match with food than reds.

Light Whites

19

GENERICS—California Chablis, California dry sauterne (so-tern), California White Burgundy

VARIETALS—Emerald Riesling, Green Hungarian, Grey Riesling, Folle Blanche, Sylvaner (Sil-*vah*-ner) (also known as Sylvaner Riesling or just Riesling), Traminer (Trah-*mee*-ner)

Light white wines are refreshing but unobtrusive, somewhat in the way a Delicious apple is crisp and clean but not notably flavorful. This may sound like a backhanded compliment, but the quality of light whites becomes admirable when a meal of chicken or seafood is so delicately flavored itself that most wines would overwhelm the food. Having such restrained character makes these wines versatile.

For the same reasons, these wines make excellent choices for use in the cooking of almost all white-wine-flavored dishes. Only rarely does a dish demand one of the highly flavored white wines.

California Chablis

The white counterpart to California Burgundy, California Chablis covers the same ground that "white wine"—it has no other name—covers in France. That is to say, there is no particular limit to what grape varieties may be used in the making, but the end result is almost always dry or just off-dry, the kind of wine people drink without second thoughts when they are having ordinary family dinners.

If a Chablis belongs to any one of the widely distributed labels in this country, it will be sound, soft, just a shade less than dry, and a more than agreeable companion to most of the dinners served in the course of a year. If the producer is one of the big firms in California's Great Central Valley, the wine is likely to be slightly sweeter and substantially less expensive than if the label belongs to a winery in one of the state's coastal valleys. Personal preference for the individual style of one wine maker is the only way to choose one Chablis over another.

Mountain white is another term for Chablis.

California Dry Sauterne

Usually priced at $1.50 or less, this sauterne barely differs from California Chablis. However, a few wineries in the coastal valleys—especially in Livermore and the Napa Valley—use ample amounts of a highly flavored grape called Semillon to make a wine under this name. This dry sauterne makes instant friends or enemies, for the perfumy smell of Semillon does not leave people neutral. In either case dry sauterne can be a great accompaniment to poultry.

California White Burgundy

This name appears on only a handful of labels. Almost certainly a wine so labeled will be drier and sharper than a typical Chablis, making it particularly well suited for serving with white fish.

Emerald Riesling

This wine is just beginning to emerge with its own identity. It comes from a grape that was developed at the University of California to grow in California's hot Great Central Valley and produce Riesling-type wines. (Grape varieties are more narrowly acclimated than rose bushes. The *traditional* Riesling grapes evolved in the cool northerly climes of Germany and will grow only in the cooler regions of coastal California.)

The available bottlings of Emerald Riesling from the Great Central Valley wineries closely resemble wines labeled as Sylvaner, or just plain Riesling, from coastal vineyards. They are delicately flavored, are just a bit less than bone dry, and have an extraordinary affinity for buckets of steamed clams and mussels.

Folle Blanche

One grape from which French Cognac is made, Folle Blanche, makes a clean, crisp, dry white wine at one California winery, Louis M. Martini. It may be the best wine in the United States for white fish.

Green Hungarian

This wine is rather hard to distinguish from typical California Chablis, partly because a lot of Green Hungarian grapes go into Chablis blends around the state and partly because this variety is hard to distinguish from several others. Unless the label says the wine was bottled in Mission San Jose, where it is made quite sweet, use the wine as you would Chablis and you will fare well.

Grey Riesling

Not of the Riesling family of grapes at all, this wine is made from a grape named Chauché Gris, which originated in the Loire Valley in France. Soft and mildly flavored, Grey Riesling does nicely with cold chicken at early summer picnics.

21

Sylvaner

Also known as Sylvaner Riesling and just plain Riesling, this wine too often remains overlooked. Connoisseurs divide varietal white wines into the greats—Chardonnay, Johannisberg Riesling—and the less greats—all the rest, including Sylvaner. Sylvaner seems somehow to have been hidden more thoroughly than most of the other less greats.

Sylvaner does have a less distinctive character than Johannisberg Riesling, but it is similar, and it costs a good deal less than its nobler brethren. Good California Sylvaner offers a clean, round, fruity flavor that goes well with poultry, clams, crab, and sole in all their forms.

Traminer

From a grape developed in Alsace, Traminer greatly resembles Sylvaner and/or Emerald Riesling and serves the same broad range of purposes. Only three or four wineries, from counties around San Francisco Bay, offer this wine, although a good many more offer the far more forceful wine called Gewürztraminer (see the section on fruity white wines).

Fruity Whites

GENERICS—California Rhine, native grape Rhine, native grape Chablis

VARIETALS—Chenin Blanc (Scheh-nin Blan) (also known as Pineau de la Loire and White Pinot), Gewürztraminer (Gay-voortz-trah-mee-ner), Johannisberg Riesling (also known as White Riesling), Semillon (Seh-mee-yon); native grape Duchess, native grape Niagara

Ripe fruit tastes rich and sweet. So do these white wines. We do not mean to say that all fruity whites taste alike. Far from that, they have pronounced individual characters.

Because of their highly defined flavors, these wines are the most likely among the whites to be a disappointment if they are paired with an inappropriate food. Yet they produce the deepest of pleasures when combined perfectly with food. For these reasons many of the fruity white wines recommended in the recipe chapters specify the individual producers as well as the variety.

Fruity whites should be drunk as soon as possible, for the more time that separates a wine from the vintage, the less fruity it becomes. Since the charm of the wines is the fruity taste, they should be used while fresh.

California Rhine

For people who find Chablis too sharp for their tastes, a California Rhine wine is one answer. Much the same grape varieties go into both the Rhine and the Chablis, but in the Rhine an extra degree of sweetness throws the fruity taste into clearer focus and at the same time tones down any acidic or alcoholic sharpness.

Chenin Blanc

This one walks the tightrope between being a mealtime wine and a wine for luncheon or dessert. The grape variety evolved in the Vouvray district of France, where it is used to make a rather sweet wine. California wine makers for the most part follow that style.

In our view the sweeter wines serve their noblest purpose with a bowl of fresh fruit beneath a warm sun. However, people who enjoy their wines softer than we do often choose a Chenin Blanc to go with poultry, ham, or a creamy casserole.

Once in a while a label will say "dry Chenin Blanc." Even purists can take it on faith that the wine inside will be drier than regular Chenin Blanc—dry enough, in fact, to have with poultry at dinner. Otherwise, wine from this grape is most likely to be dry, or almost dry, if it goes by its alias, White Pinot.

Gewürztraminer

This fruity white is almost an opposite to Chenin Blanc: Whereas Chenin Blanc is gentle, Gewürztraminer comes very near to biting; whereas Chenin Blanc has the soft flavors of a ripe pear, Gewürztraminer has the pungency of winter plums. In truth, a really good Gewürztraminer is spicy rather than fruity. The grape variety came to the United States from Alsace, where it has to do battle with *pâté de foie gras* and even sauerkraut.

In this book we recommend Gewürztraminer with dishes that may be served with either white wine or red and with appetizer courses more often than with main meals. It is lovable in the same way that a crusty uncle is lovable—for what it is, never for what it is not.

Johannisberg Riesling

Bridging the gap between Chenin Blanc and Gewürztraminer, Johannisberg Riesling is neither as gentle as the one nor as pungent as the other. It also has a sweet, berrylike flavor that is different from that of either of the others. It is this berryish quality that makes it one of the most refreshing of California white wines. Never completely dry, never cloyingly sweet, a Johannisberg Riesling adapts to picnics and formal dinners with equal ease. Somehow, cold cracked crab seems to make the quintessential companion for this wine.

Nearly all the fine Johannisberg Rieslings come from California's Napa Valley, but Sonoma and Monterey county wineries produce good ones, too. Washington State wines from this grape show excellent character, and New York State also produces a Johannisberg Riesling.

Semillon

For one reason or another, this white wine has never become popular. Perhaps its flavors are too pronounced to be widely enjoyed. People who like their first bottle of Semillon continue to like it while those who do not like their first taste never learn to take any pleasure in the wine. When it is good, it is very good indeed with poultry, veal, and casseroles.

The Semillon grape is the one that makes French sauternes as sweet as they are. (Another one, Sauvignon Blanc, lends pungency. See the section on full-dry whites for further notes.)

Native Grape Chablis and Rhine

Wines called Chablis and Rhine that are made from native American grape varieties share with all other native grape wines a certain basic flavor, usually called "foxy" in wine books. The source of *foxy* as an adjective applied to wine is obscure, but in effect a wine is foxy when it has something akin to the awesomely specific flavor of Concord grapes. Typically, Chablis is drier than Rhine.

Dutchess and Niagara

The grape, Dutchess, often is used to make Rhine wine. It is also used to produce a wine of similar character under its own name. More rarely, the native grape Niagara produces varietal white wines with a pungency and sweetness similar to that of Dutchess wine. We find these wines more pleasant to sip than to serve with meals, but people who grow up with them enjoy them as companions to both fish and poultry.

Full-Dry Whites

VARIETALS—Chardonnay, Pinot Blanc, Sauvignon Blanc

Only a few white wines make people think of wine first and fruit second. More often than not, experts describe the full-dry white wines as austere. As accompaniments to food, they lend a note of restraint to the richness of lobster, salmon, and velvety cream sauces.

In spite of their strongly distinctive flavors, these wines are versatile because they are dry.

Chardonnay

The Chardonnay grape is the same variety used to make the great white Burgundies of France. Performing in California very much as it does in France, the grape produces the titan of California white wines, especially when it comes from the Napa Valley. In fact some of the finest California Chardonnays have fooled wine makers from Burgundy, as well as other experts, in blind tastings.

In spite of its authenticated greatness, Chardonnay is a wine that many novices find hard to admire. It is aged in almost the same way that great red wines are, and like them, it develops a strong, almost biting character. It is, logically enough, almost always the favorite white wine of the dyed-in-the-wool Cabernet Sauvignon fanciers.

Current prices demand that a Chardonnay be reserved for an especially elegant dinner, such as Maine lobster or Thanksgiving turkey.

Pinot Chardonnay is wine made from the very same grape. Both names exist because of a long-standing botanic confusion about the grape variety's family ties.

Pinot Blanc

This wine can be compared to Chardonnay in very much the same way that Sylvaner can be compared to Johannisberg Riesling. They are not quite the same wine, but the similarities are many, and the Pinot Blanc's price is more reasonable. Novices who find Chardonnay too much to take may well think Pinot Blanc an even better wine.

Sauvignon Blanc

Ranging from bone dry to uncommonly sweet, Sauvignon Blanc goes by three names in the process, the other two being **Blanc Fumé** (Blan Fumay) and **Fumé Blanc.**

The essential flavor of the namesake grape is not generously fruity but almost herblike. For this reason it is almost always blended with a softer grape. The truly dry Sauvignon Blancs tend to be dominated by the namesake grape, with only small percentages of other varieties blended in for softening. The sweeter ones are likely to have slightly higher percentages of blend grapes.

When Sauvignon Blanc is truly dry—and the label will say that it is—it makes a superb accompaniment to fish. When the wine is just a shade off-dry, it goes well with fish but even better with poultry or veal. Most of the off-dry bottlings are labeled Blanc Fumé or Fumé Blanc.

Several wineries offer Sauvignon Blanc as a frankly sweet wine to go with light desserts. The grape performs very well in the role. Once again, the labels are honest on the point, indicating whether the wine is medium-dry or sweet.

Incidentally, a tasting of six or seven wines from this grape can demonstrate clearly that sweet is not an absolute matter. The degree of sweetness retained in a wine can be calibrated on a fine scale. Experts speak of wines as being bone dry, dry, off-dry, medium-dry, medium-sweet, sweet, and positively ghastly. There is a Sauvignon Blanc to support every shading but the last one.

Seyval Blanc

One of the newest varietal wines from French-American hybrid grapes, Seyval Blanc is symptomatic of the steadily expanding roster of New York State wines as growers look for ways to broaden their audience to include European-oriented wine drinkers.

Seyval Blanc is made dry, or just off-dry. Its fruit flavors have been likened to the apple-ish tastes of Chardonnay, although its overall character is less austere.

Sweet Whites

GENERICS—Haut sauterne (Oh so-tern), sweet sauterne, Chateau (Sha-toe) (that is, Chateau LaSalle, Chateau Concannon, etc., *chateau* having come to mean "sweet" on an American wine label)

VARIETALS—Muscat Canelli, Moscato, Malvasia Bianca; from French-American hybrids: Aurora

26

The line between wine for dinner and wine for dessert shifts and wavers, depending as it does on personal taste. Many people think of Chenin Blanc as being sweet enough to go with dessert. The wines categorized here are a good deal sweeter than the sweetest Chenin Blanc. The vast majority of people who know these wines drink them with a dessert such as unfrosted pound cake or with a bowl of fresh fruit in a sunny garden.

The generics are, like all generic wines, blended so that no one grape variety comes through as the dominating flavor. Inexpensive, the generics are intended for casual use.

The Muscat varietals, on the other hand, taste much like the big green Muscat grapes you buy fresh in the grocery store. (A note of caution: Some of the Muscat wines are made as both 12-percent- and 20-percent-alcohol wines under the same names; the ones with the higher alcohol content do not provide the same refreshing drink.)

Aurora wine, from New York, is as specific in its way as any Muscat.

This category also should include sweet Semillon and sweet Sauvignon Blanc. (For fuller descriptions of the characters of these varietals, see the entries on Semillon, in the section on fruity whites, and on Sauvignon Blanc, under full-dry whites.)

America's White Wines

Generics

Chablis
Dry Sauterne
Haut Sauterne
Mountain White

Rhine Wine
Sweet Sauterne
White Burgundy

Varietals

Chardonnay
  (also known as Pinot Chardonnay)
Chenin Blanc
  (also known as White Pinot,
    Pineau de la Loire)
Emerald Riesling
Flora
Folle Blanche
Franken Riesling
French Colombard
Gewürztraminer
Green Hungarian
Grey Riesling
Johannisberg Riesling
  (also known as White Riesling)

Malvasia Bianca
Muscadelle du Bordelais
Muscat Canelli
Pinot Blanc
Sauvignon Blanc
  (also known as Blanc Fumé,
    Fumé Blanc)
Semillon
Sweet Semillon
Sylvaner
  (also known as
    Sylvaner Riesling, Riesling)
Traminer

27

Native or Hybrid Varietals

Aurora
Catawba
Delaware

Diamond
Niagara
Seyval Blanc

4

Other American Wines

Although this book is concerned primarily with America's red and white table wines, it would be an unhappy mistake to overlook the three other classes of wine—sparkling, appetizer, and dessert. All are amply represented on the lists of American wine producers and in the cellars of sage connoisseurs. Between them, they offer attractive ways to launch meals and to cap them.

Sparkling Wines

Sparkling wines have many of the characteristics of table wines. They range from white to red, from dry to sweet, from young to old. Their alcohol level is similar, too, at 11 to 12 percent.

The difference is that they have bubbles, which somehow adds a note of festivity that no other wine can offer. The consumption of sparkling wines at weddings, bon voyage parties, and brunches is appropriate not only because of the occasion but because the wine is in the company of the right foods. By and large, sparkling wines are much better with snacks and appetizers than with main courses.

Every now and then, a wine maker will produce a varietal sparkling wine; however, most sparkling wines are generic. The expensive ones are bottle-fermented, a slow and costly technique. Less expensive sparkling wines are made by a quicker, cost-saving process called "Charmat," or "bulk process." In essence, the bottle-fermented sparkling wines equate with varietal table wines, and the Charmat types with generics.

Champagne

The white wine among sparkling wines, champagne, ranges from bone dry to quite sweet. The bone-dry ones are called "Natural," or "Natur"; those labeled "Brut" also are dry, although somewhat less austere than "Natural." Both are well suited to serve as appetizers or with meals that otherwise would call for dry white wines. Champagnes labeled "Extra Dry" or "Sec" are—in spite of their names—rather sweet. They are appropriate for lawn parties, wedding receptions, and other gatherings at which conviviality is more important than food.

Sparkling Malvasia and Sparkling Muscadelle

These wines have the affable flavor of the muscat grape, from which they derive. Being sweet, they make fine desserts by themselves.

Pink Sparkling Wine

Pink sparkling wines are sweet, the old standby being pink champagne. In recent years, Cold Duck has also emerged as an overwhelmingly popular wine. Darker in hue and sweeter than pink champagne, its hallmark is the unmistakable flavor of Concord grapes. (Cold Duck, being a commercial invention, quickly spawned a whole bestiary of other cold "animals," including Bear, Hawk, Turkey, and Eagle. The names differ more than the wines do.)

The wine called "crackling rosé" is made by a slightly different method than pink champagne and is somewhat less bubbly as a result. Otherwise, they resemble each other considerably.

Red Sparkling Wine

Sparkling Burgundy is the usual appellation for red sparkling wine. Nearly all bottlings of it are light and fruity with greater or lesser degrees of sweetness. If you find a bottle of sparkling Burgundy that says "fermented in this bottle," it may prove to be a dry wine, but this is rare. Red sparkling wines are brought out at celebration dinners of prime ribs or charcoal-broiled steaks. People who take wine seriously do not like them, as a matter of principle more than as a matter of taste.

Appetizer Wines

The classic between-meals wines are sherry and dry vermouth. In recent years, "pop" wines have joined them. The three have very little in common except for their role as appetizers.

Sherry

In the United States, sherries begin as rather neutral white wines. Brandy is added, and the wines are then deliberately oxidized (caused to turn brown by exposure to air or heat, or both). The total process creates an admixture of flavors reminiscent of those of wine, wizening apples, nuts, and, sometimes, a bit of caramel. Almost no fruity or grapy flavors remain in sherries.

This latter fact also means that the differences between California sherries from vinifera grapes and other American sherries from native grapes are minimized. Experts who can easily spot native grape table wines in blind tastings have a far harder time distinguishing New York, Ohio, and Arkansas sherries.

Appetizer sherries, meant to be taken in small sips from small glasses as a prelude to dinner, range from very dry to moderately sweet. The dry ones are labeled "dry," "pale," or "cocktail." Sherries that taste a bit sweeter but still perform well as appetizers are labeled "sherry"—no more, no less. A sherry labeled "Palomino" is varietal, from the grape of that name. (Dessert sherries, mentioned in the next section, carry labels with such names as "Cream Sherry," "Triple Cream," or a similar variation. They are very sweet.)

Dry Vermouth

Vermouths are white wines infused with proprietary formulas of herbs and aromatics. Some taste fresh and flowery; others have a dry, almost weedy pungency. Americans accustomed to drinking dry martinis have a difficult time imagining vermouth as a drink in its own right, but it is a good one, especially over ice on warm evenings.

Incidentally, if a dry vermouth seems too pungent, add a twist of lemon to sharpen its fruity qualities.

"Pop" Wines

Flavored wines burst into favor in the United States during the latter half of the 1960s when large-scale wineries in the Central Valley of California started using flavoring agents that earlier had been reserved for soda pop. These flavoring agents include cola, citrus, tropical fruits, berries, and the like. A neutral wine (usually white, sometimes red) merely serves as a vehicle for the added flavoring. The effect is more or less that of a premixed punch. Because these beverages taste altogether unlike traditional wines, they are scorned by purists. However, a good punch is a good punch, and some of these beverages are estimable on that basis.

All the "pop" wines use proprietary names that try to convey an impression of the taste. For example, the ones patterned after Spanish Sangria are called Spañada and Sangrole. A variation on planter's punch that uses tropical fruits goes by the name Key Largo.

Individually, these wines have tended to be faddish. Dozens of labels have already come and gone. But as a type, they are prospering. The oldest "pop" wine originated in France and goes by the name Dubonnet.

Dessert Wines

The dessert wines—with alcohol levels between 17 and 20 percent—are meant less to complement other sweets than to replace them. The traditional food accompaniments, if any, are pound cake, unfrosted cookies, and nuts.

American dessert wines have been getting better and better in recent years. As a class, they were not as good in the years before the 1960s, and vast numbers of people lost interest. Many of the disenchanted would be amazed at what is now available throughout the price range, especially among the Tinta Ports, tawny ports, and cream sherries.

Grapes for nearly all California dessert wines grow in the great Central Valley, regardless of where the wine is bottled. Warmer than the coastal regions, the interior valley produces the extra ripeness in grapes that leads to good sweet wine. Elsewhere in the United States, good dessert wine depends on the wine makers's choosing the naturally sweetest of the native grape varieties.

The principal choice among dessert wines is between fresh, fruity flavors and aged ones. If the color of the wine is white or bright red, the flavor is likely to be quite fresh and fruitlike. If the color is amber or tawny red, the flavor of the wine probably will be dominated by the tastes of age. (When a wine has strong brown tones, it has been oxidized, and oxidation produces the most obvious aged tastes in all wines.)

The pale-hued, and thus fruity-tasting, dessert wines are represented principally by white port and Malvasia Bianca. White ports are extremely sweet and almost always marked by the distinctive flavor of the Muscat grape. Malvasia Bianca is usually a little less sweet than white port but otherwise tastes much the same because Malvasia grapes belong to the Muscat family.

Ruby-hued dessert wines are to pale dessert wines as red table wines are to white ones. They have somewhat more bite because fermentation extracted some tannins from the skins and seeds of the grapes. The major types are ruby port, Tinta port, and Black Muscat. Ruby port is a thorough-going generic, made from whatever blend of grapes the wine maker chooses. (Frequently, the California choice is superripe Zinfandel grapes, which make excellent dessert wine.) Tinta port is a varietal in the sense that one or more red grapes of the varieties used in making Portuguese ports go into the wine; it is the most prestigious and most costly of California ports. Black Muscat comes from one of the black grapes in the muscat family. The change of hue does not disguise the grape's basic flavor.

The tawny dessert wines come from pale-hued grapes and are then darkened with either heat or great age as is done with sherry. The names of the wines are Angelica, cream sherry, Marsala, Muscatel, and tawny port. Except for Marsala, which tastes like raisins, and Muscatel, which tastes of muscat grapes, there is no sharp line dividing the tawny dessert wines. Suffice to say that the combination of sweet taste with oxidized bouquet can produce enormously complex impressions, the kind that keep one sipping very slowly and thoughtfully for a long time on one small glass. These wines are fine not only as dessert but also as relaxers before bedtime.

America's Sparkling, Appetizer and Dessert Wines

Sparkling

Champagne Brut
Champagne Extra Dry
Champagne Natural
Champagne Sec

Pink Champagne
Cold Duck
Sparkling Burgundy

Appetizer

Cocktail Sherry
Dry Sherry

Medium-dry Sherry
Vermouth (Dry, Sweet)

Dessert

Angelica
Black Muscat
Cream Sherry
Madeira
Marsala
Muscatel

Muscat Frontignan
Ruby Port
Tawny Port
Tinta Port
Tokay
White Port

5

America's Wineries

In a typical year, the total production of wine in the United States is about 250 million gallons, and this figure is growing as fast as new vines can be planted. Of that total, California vineyards yield about 215 million gallons. New York produces about 23 million. The remaining 22 million gallons divide among twenty-five other states.

Close to three hundred wineries actively court the growing American wine market, and they are increasing in number, too, as vineyard acreage expands. Each winery offers from three to thirty different wines. A novice in a liquor store finds the profusion of wine labels bewildering. A brief lesson in geography simplifies the choices at least as much as knowing all the types of wine described in the preceding chapters.

California's Central Valley

From Lodi south to Bakersfield, a distance of 220 miles, the fertile Central Valley of California accounts for more than half the vineyard acreage in the United States and for nearly all the truly large wineries.

Historically, the greatest production here has been of appetizer and dessert wines because the grape varieties that go into these wines thrive in the valley's long, dry summers.

In recent years, however, the balance of production has swung sharply to table wines. New strains of vinifera grapes developed for the warm climate by the University of California at Davis seem to have provided the impetus. Improved vineyard management of all grapes and improved wine-making techniques have allowed the shift to progress at remarkable speed.

At this point, while more acres are being planted in finer grapes and more wineries are improving their equipment, the severest wine critics in England, and even some in France, think that the Central Valley already produces the world's best table wine for daily use at a low price.

The acknowledged leader is the firm of E. & J. Gallo in Modesto, which makes and sells far more wine than any competitor anywhere. The closest challenger is Heublein's United Vintners, which has as primary labels Italian Swiss Colony and Jacques Bonet. Considerably smaller companies, but still major factors in the market, are Franzia, in Ripon, and Guild, which has several wineries stretching the length of the valley. Guild labels include Winemaster, Famiglia Cribari and Roma. With the exception of Franzia, these companies harvest grapes both in the San Joaquin and in the coastal regions in order to offer a diversity of wines at modest prices—almost always between one and two dollars a bottle.

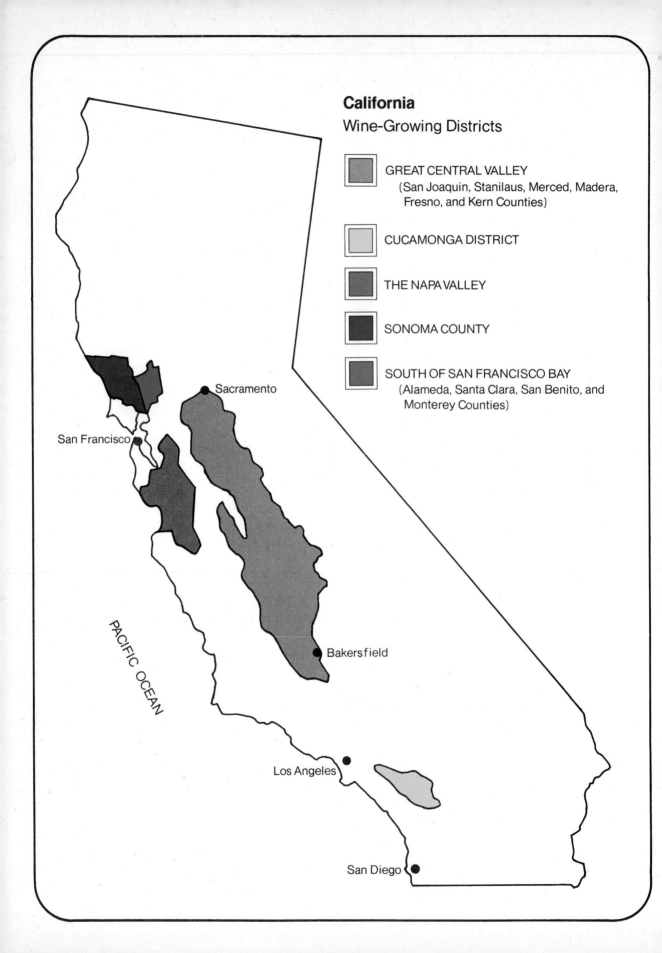

California

Wine-Growing Districts

GREAT CENTRAL VALLEY
   (San Joaquin, Stanilaus, Merced, Madera,
Fresno, and Kern Counties)

CUCAMONGA DISTRICT

THE NAPA VALLEY

SONOMA COUNTY

SOUTH OF SAN FRANCISCO BAY
   (Alameda, Santa Clara, San Benito, and
Monterey Counties)

Sacramento

San Francisco

PACIFIC OCEAN

Bakersfield

Los Angeles

San Diego

Nearly all table wines under these labels are generics. There is never a truly dry wine among these, but some of the Chablis and Burgundies come close to being dry. The wineries still offer their traditional appetizer and dessert wines. They also provide increasing amounts of "bulk process" sparkling wines, and, finally, huge volumes of the flavored "pop" wines.

A considerable number of smaller wineries prosper in the Central Valley, especially around the town of Lodi, and from these wineries a whole new range of varietal table wines is beginning to flow. Many are from the grape varieties developed at the University of California; prime among them are Ruby Cabernet (a cousin of Cabernet Sauvignon) and Emerald Riesling (a relative of Johannisberg Riesling). Other wines from the traditional varieties are Chenin Blanc, French Colombard, and Semillon, among whites, and Barbera from the reds. The reds are likely to be dry and the whites off-dry.

The companies offering these varietal wines include Barengo, Bear Mountain (under the M. LaMont label), California Growers, and East-Side (under the Royal Host and Pastene labels). They also offer well-made generic table wines and appetizer and dessert wines. Prices for wines from these wineries tend to range between two and three dollars. Bottles are not to be found on every store shelf as are those from the truly large companies.

Several other wineries in the Central Valley do not market wines directly but sell in bulk to bottlers in other parts of the country. Some of these wines find their way into blends with native grape wines. Some are sold as California wines. The small type at the bottom of the label will indicate if the wine was shipped in bulk and bottled outside California.

Cucamonga

East of Los Angeles lies an old wine district that shrinks steadily under urban pressure. Only two companies continue to make and sell wine from local grapes: One is Brookside; the other is Original Cucamonga (which uses Chateau Chambord and Original Romano as labels). Quality and price make these firms competitive with the small wineries of the Central Valley.

California's Coastal Valleys

From the counties surrounding San Francisco Bay come the most prestigious, most expensive, and rarest California wines. In these valleys is the American continent's closest known approximation of the climates of the classic wine-growing districts of Europe. As a result the wines closely resemble their European counterparts.

The Napa Valley, north of San Francisco, is the best known and thus far most diligent competition for excellent European wines. Napa's neighbor to the west, Sonoma County, and the several counties south of San Francisco Bay do not lag far behind; the south-bay counties include Alameda, Monterey, San Benito, and Santa Clara. Nearly all California's acreage of Cabernet Sauvignon, Pinot Noir, Chardonnay, and Johannisberg Riesling is to be found in this general region.

The focus is inevitably upon varietal table wines, although most producers also offer generic wines and appetizer and dessert wines. A few specialize in sparkling wines. The most prestigious varietals tend to cost from $4 to $10; none costs less than $2.25.

Any list of wines from the coast counties confers some built-in frustration on people living outside California, Chicago, Dallas, New York City, and Washington, D.C., because some percentage of the list will not be readily available. This is not all bad news, however. At some point, everyone who drinks wine with pleasure should visit a winery to see that good wine comes from the hard toil of honest men. Most coast county wineries are built on a scale that makes the art of wine making understandable when you look at the equipment. In addition, the wineries provide tasting rooms, where an inquisitive visitor with a week on his hands may sample several hundred dollars' worth of splendid wines—wines he would otherwise have to buy to taste, *if* he could find them.

Napa Valley

Though it produces only 10 percent of California's wine, the Napa Valley looks the way wine country is supposed to look. For much of the valley's twenty-five-mile length, elegant old estates punctuate its fifteen-thousand-acre carpet of vines. Most of the estates date to the 1880s and 1890s, when California wines enjoyed an earlier prestige. Beaulieu, Beringer, Inglenook, and Charles Krug all are names dating from that era. Now, in the 1960s and 1970s, as wine making flourishes again, a second generation of estate names has been born in the valley, including Chappellet, Heitz, Robert Mondavi, Souverain, and Sterling. In all, there are forty wineries active in the valley, with more planned.

The Christian Brothers, Beringer/Los Hermanos, and Inglenook are the easiest labels to find in the rest of the country. All three have extensive vineyard holdings in the Napa Valley and supplement these with grapes purchased in other districts. Beaulieu, Charles Krug, Louis M. Martini, and Robert Mondavi are substantially smaller but are still likely to be represented at good wine merchants in any sizable city in the United States. The wineries smaller than these—Chappellet, Heitz Cellars, Oakville Vineyards, and Souverain—have extremely limited distribution; their products are usually found in only select stores in major cities.

Two other valley wineries, Hanns Kornell and Schramsberg, concentrate on sparkling wines. Kornell is as large as Beaulieu; Schramsberg fits the Chappellet group for volume.

The rest of the Napa Valley wineries have virtually no distribution. For example, Stony Hill sells all its legendary white wine at the winery. Other cellars—including Chateau Montelena, Spring Mountain, and Sterling—are too young to have much wine on the market yet.

Sonoma County

Though its vine acreage is almost identical to the Napa Valley's, Sonoma County extends over a far larger landscape. Only a handful of the county's prestigious wineries enjoy distribution outside California—Buena Vista, Korbel, Pedroncelli, Sebastiani, and Windsor (also known as Tiburon and Sonoma Vineyards). All are approximately the size of Beaulieu, Martini, and others of that scale in the Napa Valley.

Buena Vista and Sebastiani are located in the old Spanish pueblo town of Sonoma, at the south end of the county just across the bay from San Francisco. The others form a ring around the town of Healdsburg in the Russian River Valley. A rapidly growing wine district, this area will soon have another half-dozen wineries.

Sonoma County is also headquarters for the huge Italian Swiss Colony and a raft of anonymous or nearly anonymous bulk wineries. Italian Swiss Colony uses Sonoma County grapes but also draws heavily on Central Valley vineyards. (Central Valley wineries, in turn, buy great amounts of Sonoma wine from the bulk producers for blending into their generic table wines.)

Alameda, Santa Clara, San Benito, and Monterey Counties

Because of population pressures, vineyard locations south of San Francisco Bay have been shifting greatly since the late 1950s. Before then, Alameda County, including the Livermore Valley, and Santa Clara County were major vineyard districts; Wente is the famous name in Livermore, while Almaden and Paul Masson dominate Santa Clara. These firms and another Santa Clara winery called Mirassou Vineyards have shifted most of their vines but not their wineries south to San Benito and Monterey counties in the past fifteen years. The future of the region is with these two counties, which already bear the larger half of the region's total acreage.

Still, the historical home districts of these firms have not been rubbed out. Wente maintains sizable vineyards in Livermore. A small but prestigious neighbor there is Concannon Vineyard.

Almaden and Paul Masson maintain their bases in Santa Clara County, as does Mirassou. The Novitiate of Los Gatos also has vineyards and a winery in the neighborhood, whose center is the city of San Jose. Though its holdings are much smaller than either Almaden's or Masson's, the Novitiate produces enough to be represented in most major American cities.

Yet another winery, Weibel, has its home halfway between San Jose and Livermore but is building a new winery in Mendocino County, 130 miles north of San Francisco. Weibel specializes in sparkling wines.

A last bastion of the old-fashioned country winery is found around the town of Gilroy in Santa Clara County. The places bear names such as Live Oaks, Bertero, Uvas, Fortino, and Kruse, and they make good, honest wine at low prices. There is only one hitch: You almost have to buy it at the door. But doing so restores one's perspective.

New York State

The biggest wine-producing area outside California is New York's Finger Lakes district, the heart of which is Hammondsport at the tip of Lake Keuka. As in California, most wineries in the area welcome visitors, offering them tours and tastings.

Most of the old vineyards in New York are planted with the native grapes or hybrids based upon them, and most of the wines are of this type. However, French-American hybrids, and even *Vitis vinifera,* are being experimented with more and more and are producing wine for distribution.

The native grapes include Catawba, Delaware, Isabella, Moore's Diamond, and Vergennes, as well as the inevitable Concord. The French-American hybrids,which used to be known by a complex number system, are most easily recognized these days by three representatives: Aurora, Baco Noir, and Chelois.

Taylor Wine Company in the Finger Lakes region is by far the largest New York winery. That makes it middle-sized by California standards. Taylor production ranges across the five classes of wine, all of which are derived from native American grapes. A subsidiary of Taylor, Great Western, produces wines from both native and French-American hybrids. The label is most famous for its sparkling wines, but the recent additions of Baco Noir, Chelois, and Aurora to its list may change that reputation.

Gold Seal and Widmer's, also located in the Finger Lakes district, follow the Taylor example, concentrating their production in wines made of native

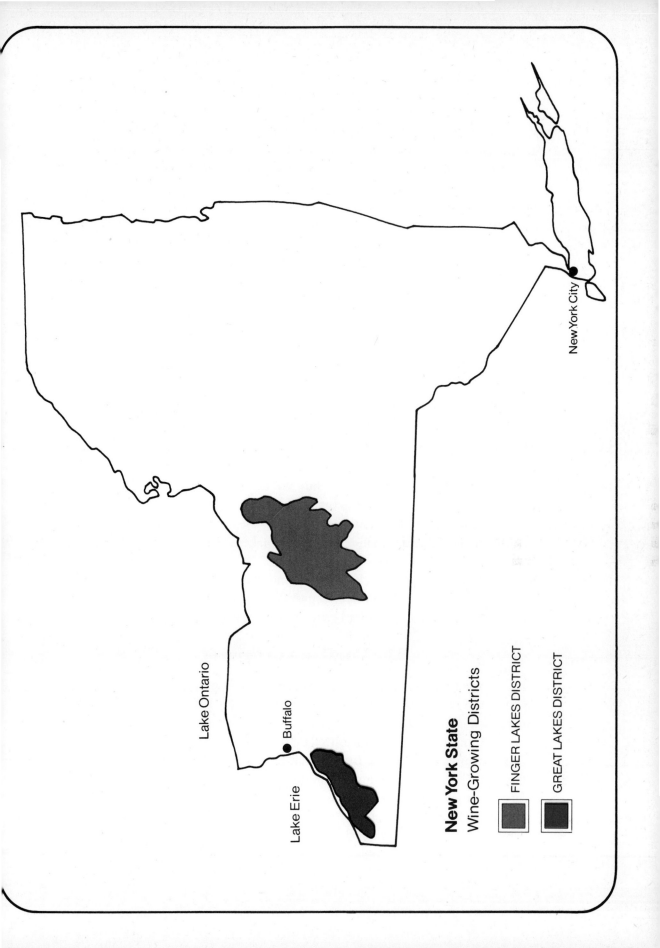

New York State
Wine-Growing Districts

FINGER LAKES DISTRICT

GREAT LAKES DISTRICT

New York City

Lake Ontario

Buffalo

Lake Erie

grapes. Widmer's goes farther and offers mostly varietals. The wines are in fairly wide distribution east of the Rockies.

Two relatively new wineries in the Finger Lakes district have staked a great deal on the French-American hybrids. They are Bully Hill and Boordy.

Boordy, to be specific, is only partly in the Finger Lakes. It is an outgrowth of an experimental vineyard in Maryland maintained for years by an ingenious—or maybe genius—vineyardist named Philip Wagner. In its New York operations, Boordy grows French-American hybrid grapes in vineyards near Westfield, in the western part of the state, and makes them into wine at a winery near Penn Yan on Lake Keuka. (There is yet another Boordy on the opposite side of the country, near Yakima, Washington. It is noted in the Pacific Northwest section.)

Bully Hill is the property of Walter Taylor, Jr., who parted company with the Taylor Wine Company to make wines from the hybrid grapes on his own.

Both Boordy and Bully Hill started out with short lists of generics forthrightly named red, white, and rosé. Both have quickly moved into varietals from their hybrids, some of them vintage-dated.

Konstantin Frank is the only producer of wine from vinifera grapes in New York. He sticks to his appointed tasks in the Finger Lakes region no matter what people say about vinifera being impossible to grow there profitably. The operation is minuscule, but the hopes remain enormous. Frank makes mostly Johannisberg Riesling and Chardonnay.

There are a handful of other wineries in the Finger Lakes region, notably Oh-Neh-Dah and Canandaigua. Both make generics using native grape species.

Down on the Hudson, High Tor Vineyard has been a leader in the selection of French-American hybrid grapes for growing. Because of its limited production, its wine is hard to find though, even close by.

The Pacific Northwest

The state of Washington long has been a grower of native American grapes in its fertile central plain. More recently, producers have begun to explore the French-American hybrids and also the classic vinifera species.

Washington has never measured up to New York or Ohio as a producer of wines from native grapes. But the Yakima Valley, on the dry eastern foothills of the Cascade Mountain Range, already has proved itself a better adapted home for vinifera, and threatens to surpass New York with the quality of its wines from hybrid vines.

The vinifera producer in the state is Ste. Michelle, a division of the same

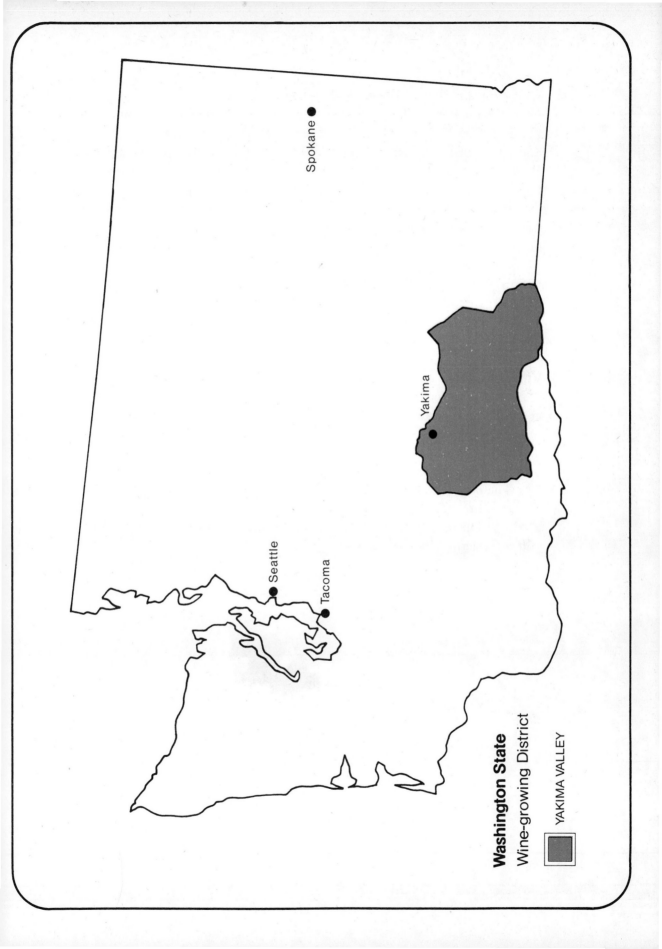

Washington State
Wine-growing District

YAKIMA VALLEY

wine company that produces native wines for local consumption under the Nawico and Pomerelle labels. Its most esteemed wines are Johannisberg Riesling, Semillon, and Grenache. The French-American and vinifera producer is Boordy, the same firm that also operates a winery in New York. Boordy's generic white is just called white; the vinifera white wines include Riesling and Chardonnay.

It is a measure of the success of these firms that both ship wines to California. Earlier Washington wines never had been sold out of state in the ninety years of their existence.

Oregon does not at this point have a truly commercial wine industry, but promising small vineyards are in production near McMinnville (mostly Chardonnay and Pinot Noir) and Roseburg (mostly Johannisberg Riesling).

The Other States

Vineyards grow and people make wine wherever the climate allows. As more and more people accept wine on their dinner tables, the number of vineyards proliferates.

At least twenty-five states besides California, New York, and Washington have at least one winery in business as of the moment. With very few exceptions, the wineries are small and limited to very local distribution.

The major exceptions are Meier's in Ohio, Bronte in Michigan, and Wiederkehr in Arkansas. Wines under these labels reach a number of markets some distance from home. They do because they taste good. Should you come across a bottle, have a try.

Champagne Peaches, p. 152, and Ported Blueberries Sundae, p. 154

6

Buying, Storing, and Serving Wine

At this point, after a long catalog of winery names has followed a long catalog of wine types, the prospect of choosing the "right" wine may seem overwhelming. It is not.

Buying Wine for the Home

Getting a small, serviceable cellar together is truly a simple matter. As we proposed in Chapter 1, a newcomer should first buy two cases of moderately priced, everyday wine—one case of red, one of white—and then drink these at a steady rate with ordinary family meals. This will make you a genuine expert in two wines, and give you a basis for thinking about others.

While still drinking from the two cases, pick up occasional single bottles of other, similar reds and whites, and measure these against the wines in the cases. If you come across something better for the same money, change brands when you buy a replacement case for the first one. It's not a bad idea even to keep a few notes on single bottles of wine that you try and like so that you'll remember when you visit the liquor store.

An experienced wine drinker can make a good core cellar with just four wines: the inexpensive red for daily drinking, a more expensive red for company, and a similar pair of whites.

It is always a pleasure to think of a lady we know who lives on the outskirts of Brussels, Belgium, who buys two wines every year—700 bottles of the same red, and 700 bottles of the same white—from the same winery in Burgundy. Of course, she is in her seventies and is entitled to having made up her mind.

Still, an experimental soul will occasionally pick up bottles of other wines to see whether he should be branching out and to keep his perspective clear. In some states, it is worth buying these peripheral wines in lots of a dozen in order to obtain a 10-percent discount. (In many states the discount applies only to wines from one winery and sometimes only to a solid case of one type.)

The peripheral wines should mostly be first-rate varietals and reflect your personal interests in food. For example, anyone who eats a great deal of seafood should pick up dry white wines when they are a good buy. Somebody who dotes on lamb should always have a weather eye cocked for well-aged, or age-worthy reds. Thoughts along these lines are explored in considerable detail in the recipe chapters, where our favorite choices are listed by type and brand, with each recipe calling for a beverage wine.

But the main purpose of a small cellar is to have a wine ready to serve that you know you like.

Anyone who is setting out to become a full-fledged wine hobbyist has

47

a different task. While the casual drinker wants a steady supply of the one Pinot Noir he favors, the hobbyist wants to lay in representative samples of a dozen or more, because comparison is what makes wine a superb hobby. A representative sample is six or more bottles. The hobbyist acquires wine as rapidly as his budget allows, the trick being to buy at the best available price at the earliest possible moment. An absolute maxim with red wines is that time costs money.

In recent years there has been great emphasis on wine as an investment. In the main, it is red wine. (With rare exception, white cannot be an investment because it does not last.) As we've said, anyone buying a year's supply of wine saves 10 percent—no more, no less—if he purchases case lots. The big dividends are for heavy investors who assemble complete libraries of certain wines. For example, anybody who had the foresight to start collecting Georges de Latour Cabernet Sauvignon from Beaulieu Vineyard in the 1940s, when it cost mere pennies per bottle, now has the chance to make some real profit. Even the 1961 vintage, which originally sold for $4.25, is now going for $25—when a bottle can be found.

A modest collector can do his pocketbook a great favor if he buys the wine when it is initially offered and holds on to it while the price climbs steadily. His profit is redoubled by the pleasure he feels when he realizes that his cellar goes back fifteen or twenty vintages and that he can drink a bottle worth $20 that originally cost him $3.50.

Buying Wine in a Restaurant

Restaurants with thoughtfully prepared wine lists can be good places to explore new wines.

The only thing that makes wine harder to choose in a restaurant than it is elsewhere is a human element, the waiter. Confronted with this element, people often assume one of two things: Either they are going to make an embarrassingly wrong choice (the thicker the waiter's accent, the more timid his customers), or they are going to be coerced into paying a king's ransom for something sour.

On the first point, remember that the waiter wants a generous tip, which he cannot expect from people who are angry because they have been humiliated. He is far more likely to be helpful than anything else.

On the second point, the restaurant's wine list states a price for every bottle. The list can be studied with an easy rule of thumb in mind: Pay for a full bottle of wine about what you pay for one dinner; that is, if the average price per dinner around the table runs six dollars, choose from among the wines at that price. On the other hand, if the dinner is a celebration, you may want to order a more expensive wine.

With the field narrowed by price, look for a name you know you like—any name. If, for example, you have enjoyed Louis Martini wines, look for something from Louis Martini. If you know you have enjoyed Pinot Noirs in the past, look for a Pinot Noir. If you find a Louis Martini Pinot Noir, look no further.

If there are no familiar wines on the list, confess. Tell the waiter that you do not recognize any of the wines, and ask him to recommend the one in your price range that comes closest to a wine you do know.

Most restaurants stock half bottles of wine on basis that this is the right amount for two people—and it is for two beginners or two people who have had cocktails before dinner. With experience and without cocktails, a couple can consume a full bottle of wine during a leisurely dinner. If your meal is a speedy affair, have a glass or two of the restaurant's house wine.

When wine comes to a restaurant table, the waiter usually gives the cork to the host and then pours a sample in his glass. The host is expected to assure himself that the wine is sound before any is served to the guests. The cork will not tell you anything helpful. Palm it, and indicate that the waiter should pour the sample glass. Taste that quickly, and if the wine is not overwhelmingly disagreeable, have it poured around. (We say "overwhelmingly disagreeable" because hosts often tend to be overanxious and not in a mood to enjoy the first sip.) If the wine is not fit to drink, refuse it and ask for another bottle.

49

Storing Wine

In the course of 6,000 years, wine has acquired a heavy burden of tradition. There are right ways and wrong ways to do nearly everything connected with the beverage—from the way one carries it home from the store to the way one empties the bottle.

However, the extreme rights and wrongs pertain only to extremely expensive, extremely rare wines. It is all right to make a fuss over an irreplaceable bottle of twenty-five-year-old Cabernet Sauvignon, but it is nonsense to feel bound by rules in connection with young Burgundy available everywhere at $1.50 a bottle.

This section examines the "rules" on the basis of when and when not to fret.

To Chill or Not to Chill

Chilling a bottle of wine has two somewhat contrary effects: Cold dulls the flavors in the wine itself but refreshes the palate of the drinker for other flavors.

The general rule is that white, rosé, and sparkling wines are served chilled, while red wines are served at cool room temperature. However, on hot days it is often a better idea to cool a red than to serve it at a warmer temperature. Most appetizer wines can be served cool on a hot day or warmer on a cold day. White dessert wines are generally chilled; the red and tawny ones are kept at room temperature.

More explicit conditions are as follows.

White wines White wines have more natural grape acids than other wines, making them taste sharper. Chilling quells this sharp quality just as it makes a cold orange seem less biting than a warm one. Chilling also throws the soft fruit flavors in the wine into greater prominence. A typical, young white wine seems best at a serving temperature between 48 and 55 degrees, which is reached after two to three hours in a refrigerator.

The same rules apply to rosés.

With age, a few exceptional whites grow softer and more complex. A person who has taken the pains to acquire an older white wine will appreciate the wine more when it has been only lightly cooled. Thus, an hour in the refrigerator is enough for a five-year-old, or older, Chardonnay, Sauvignon Blanc, or Gewürztraminer.

Sparkling wines Champagnes are fully as sharp as any other white wine and benefit from chilling in the same way. But the overwhelming reason to chill champagne and all other sparkling wines is to slow down the escape of the bubbles; the colder the wine, the slower this process is. Adequate chilling time for these wines is three hours in the refrigerator or no more than two hours in a bucket of ice.

Red wines The rule is that red wines should be served at cool room temperature—about 68 to 70 degrees. But it is a rule that calls for more breaking than the one for whites. Any inexpensive young red can afford to be several degrees cooler than 68 degrees when the outdoor temperature is more than 78 degrees.

Chilling an old and fine red, however, is downright sinful in any weather. A wine is stored for a long time to make it soft, balanced, and complex. In order to savor all such qualities of age at their fullest, serve a wine such as a six- to ten-year-old Cabernet Sauvignon or Pinot Noir at a temperature of 70 degrees.

Appetizer wines All the drier American sherries may be served at whatever temperature suits the drinker. A sherry needs only an hour in the refrigerator to make it pleasant on a warm day, or it can be served over ice fairly well. But keep the same wine warm in winter so that people coming indoors can have a bit of comfort after the cold.

The flavored wines, being frivolous by nature, are likely to taste better chilled no matter what the weather.

Dessert wines The sweet table wines—sauterne, Malvasia, and light Muscat—are characterized by fresh fruity flavors and are meant to be served, with dessert, at about 50 degrees.

The temperature of dessert wines with high alcohol content (17 to 20 percent) depends on whether the flavor is fresh or aged. The younger and less expensive the wine, the better it is to cool it. Almost any young Muscat or Muscatel can be chilled to advantage, as can white port. Ruby port can be served either cooled or at room temperature.

Tawny ports have more the flavors of age than of fruit. Because the subtlety of age always emerges best when a wine is relatively warm, any genuinely old dessert wine should be served at room temperature on a wintry night in front of a fire.

Wine Cellars at Home

There are two reasons for storing wine at home. The obvious one is convenience—to avoid special or hasty trips to a wine shop. The other part is as a hobby; that is, one can store wine long after it disappears from the market or rises astronomically in price.

A convenience cellar has between twelve and forty-eight bottles and is relatively easy to establish and maintain. So long as the wines are not meant to be kept for long years of aging, they can be stored in numerous places throughout the house and can even endure considerable buffeting for a year or two. Inexpensive wines all are made to be sturdy. All young wines, no matter how rare, have the strength of youth to protect them.

A hobby cellar, on the other hand, holds hundreds and even thousands of bottles and has to be organized with cogent attention to certain rules. The purpose, after all, is to keep the wine maturing at its minimum rate in order for it to return a maximum dividend. The profit may be mere money or sublime satisfaction; it is the latter that demands careful attention to cellar conditions, since your palate rather than your pocketbook suffers most from long-lasting carelessness.

Wine in storage for any period of time has these enemies: heat, air, light, and excessive motion.

Motion   Wine, in its complexity, needs tranquillity. Otherwise, it never seems to get quite in tune with itself. To move a bottle occasionally is fine, but to subject it to the regular kind of shaking that comes from electric motors on washing machines, pumps, and dishwashers is baleful indeed. Any storage rack should be free from the jostlings of these or other quavering machines, including city subways and heavy truck traffic.

Light   The sun's ultraviolet rays are harmful to wine; if you have ever tasted a sun-struck beer, you know what we mean. No wine should be kept where it gets daily exposure either to sunlight or to fluorescent light. (Neither do wise buyers accept bottles with sun-faded labels from a merchant.) The longer the wine is to be stored, the darker its surroundings should be—all the way to cave-black for ancient reds.

Air   Air gets into closed bottles when corks are dried and shrunken, which in turn is caused by storing bottles in a standing position. Any wine that has a cork closure should be kept on its side for long-range aging. Wine in screw-capped bottles should be kept upright, for there is the chance that long contact between the wine and the cap liner will produce an off flavor.

Heat   All the other enemies of wine are more or less absolute; heat, or rather air temperature, is far more variable.

In general, convenience storage can be in the regular temperature range of a house as long as summer temperatures do not climb into the 90-degree range and stay there. The most profitable place for a wine rack is at floor level next to a north or interior wall; these locations have the coolest, most stable temperatures. Avoid putting wine bottles near south or west walls, which take the brunt of the sun.

Incidentally, the main effect of slightly greater than optimum temperature is speeded-up aging, *not* spoilage.

When stored for a period of time, each class of wine requires its particular ideal temperature condition, as noted in the following paragraphs.

Any wine that is not going to be kept more than a year will do nicely if given no more special care than described previously. Hobby storage, on the other hand, is a business. Here are the long-term storage rules for the five classes of wine.

Sparkling wines More harm than good can come from storing sparkling wines for very long. Their principal characteristics are the bubbles of carbon dioxide and the flavors from the yeasts that produce the bubbles. Long storage inevitably causes a loss of bubbles and cannot add any yeast. However, if a sparkling wine is stored for convenience, it should be kept at a cool 55 degrees or below. Warmer temperatures free the carbon dioxide which may cause the wine to go flat.

Bottles of sparkling wine with bark corks should be stored on their sides, but ones with plastic corks fare better kept upright. The bark cork needs to stay wet; the plastic one needs as much pressure as possible.

White wines These depend principally upon freshness for their charm, a requirement that dictates very cool storage—between 55 and 60 degrees—for any white wine that is to be kept for several years. In this class, the most likely candidates for long-term storage are Chardonnays, Sauvignon Blancs, and Gewürztraminers.

53

Red wines The ideal temperature range for reds in storage is between 55 and 60 degrees. The usual candidates for lengthy cellaring—five years and longer—are Cabernet Sauvignons. Pinot Noirs and Barberas sometimes are made for lengthy storage, too.

Appetizer wines Sherries are born in warmth and do not seem to mind living in it; they can be stored at 60 to 70 degrees for several years without improvement or decline. The drier sherries are seldom meant to be kept for long aging. They arrive tasting old and oxidized to the desirable limit.

Flavored wines are not meant to be stored at all.

Dessert wines Fine ports age very well in temperatures ranging between 60 and 65 degrees. Unlike sherries, they do not depend principally upon oxidized flavors. They are more like red wines, gaining such flavors as subtle additions to their early characters. This may take years.

Good Muscatels can be treated in the same way, and so can the sweet dessert sherries.

Opening and Serving Wine

Between corks and corkscrews lies a good deal of frustration in getting wine out of bottles. The problem may be with any part of the corkscrew, the cork, or both.

The two most common types of corkscrews are the worm-and-lever and the pliable blade; there is also one novelty—the air-pressure extractor.

Worm-and-lever Various corkscrews employ the worm-and-lever principle. When purchasing a corkscrew of this type, make certain that the worm provides a substantial amount of lifting surface but does not tear up the cork and that the lever allows gentle lifting action.

The best of all possible worms, according to a scientific study, is formed of thick round wire. The spiral section should be 2.5 inches long so that it goes all the way through the cork, and the spirals should be spaced .4 of an inch apart. The tip should continue in the line of the spiral rather than changing direction in any way, and the axis should be hollow.

Auger-type worms are not very effective, especially with old or otherwise spongy corks.

As for the lever, a counterrotating spiral offers two great advantages over any other type: First, it allows a very gradual increase in pressure against a weak cork, and second, it requires little strength to operate. This last advantage also means that old sedimented bottles can be opened with less of the moving and shaking that corkscrews of other designs can cause.

Pliable blade Sometimes called the dishonest butler because it leaves no mark behind, the pliable blade cork remover tends to work most effectively on old corks, especially the very old corks that have become cemented to the bottle walls while the middle of the cork grows soft. The worm-and-lever corkscrew is likely to pull such a middle out, leaving the rest of the cork to crumble into the wine, whereas the blade device will usually not do this.

To use the pliable blade cork remover effectively, apply a constant twisting motion together with the lifting pull. It is tension on the blades that keeps them biting into the cork.

This cork remover is most likely to fail on brand new corks that have been driven tightly into place.

Air pressure cork extractors These novelties work with a needle and either a hand pump or a carbon dioxide cartridge. The needle is driven through the cork until its point is in the air space between cork and wine; then increasing pressure slowly forces the cork out of the bottle. Pressure extractors are plagued with assorted potential failures. For example, any tiny weak point in a cork offers an escape route for the air or gas, and the needles tend to bend and break under the strain of use. The safest design is a hand-powered air pump rather than a carbon-dioxide-powered model, because the latter has enough pressure to explode a bottle. Among hand pumps, the trigger-action type seems sturdier than the push-pull pump.

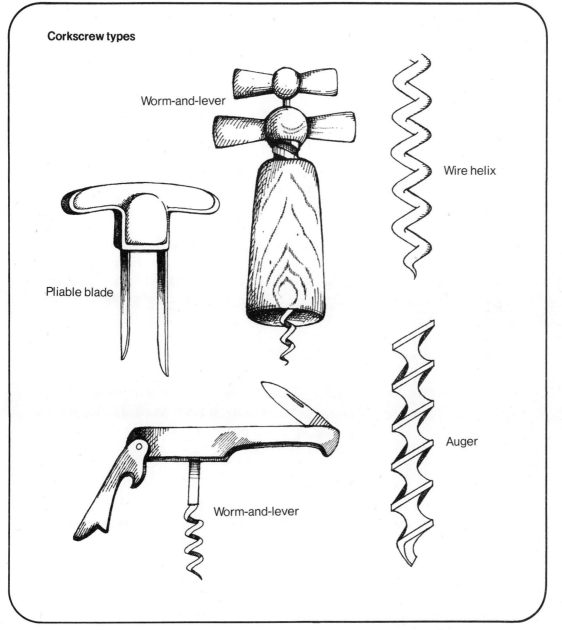

Corkscrew types

Worm-and-lever

Wire helix

Pliable blade

Auger

Worm-and-lever

Before opening a bottle of wine, it is good form to cut away the top of the foil capsule so that the wine does not touch metal when it is poured; some corkscrews have a small knife blade at one end for this purpose.

If there is some mold on the top of the cork, don't worry; it only means that a drop or two of wine was spilled on the cork when the wine was being bottled. Just wipe it away with a towel.

Opening Champagne

Because bottles of champagne and the other sparkling wines keep carbon dioxide bubbles under pressure, they do not take a regular cork. Instead, they have a cork that can fly out of the bottle as if shot from a gun. There have been some celebrated incidents of people opening champagne bottles with the corks aimed at their eyes, though fortunately, this happens rarely.

Sparkling wines *must* be opened with the cork pointed in a safe direction. Here is the step-by-step procedure.

1. Have the wine very well chilled. This reduces the effective carbon dioxide pressure.

2. With the top of the bottle pointed away from all eyes, undo and remove the wire hood, if there is one. (Some sparkling wines now have twist-off metal caps.)

3. With the bottle still pointed away from everybody and also tipped at a fairly sharp angle to create the greatest possible liquid surface (this enables gas to escape rather than allowing it to create foam), grab the top of the cork between thumb and forefinger and twist it at the same time you lift upward.

4. As soon as you hear the hiss of escaping gas, stop lifting the cork. Hold it in, if possible, to let a fair amount of gas escape before pulling out the cork completely.

5. Once the cork is out, keep the bottle tipped until it seems certain that the wine is not going to foam up and overflow. If it shows signs of foaming over, stick your thumb over the opening, or better yet, have a glass handy so that you can begin pouring immediately.

Serving Table Wine

Most of the time, wine is served in its original bottle, but there are exceptions. Half-gallon and gallon bottles of wine are unwieldy on the table. You may want to pour the wine into a carafe or decanter in the kitchen and refill as needed.

Sometimes very old wines need to be poured from the bottle before serving in order to separate the clear wine from the sediment at the bottom

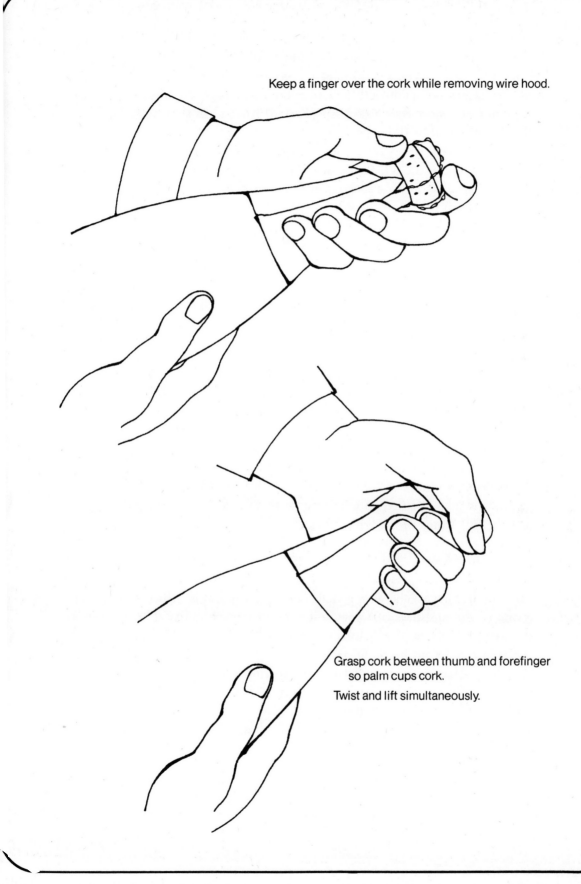

Keep a finger over the cork while removing wire hood.

Grasp cork between thumb and forefinger
so palm cups cork.

Twist and lift simultaneously.

of the bottle. Sediment may be the most healthful part of the wine, but it tastes a bit too concentrated for easy enjoyment. So a concerned host will decant the clear wine into a carafe or decanter and serve it that way. (Decanting is nothing more than a slow, steady pouring that minimizes the sloshing of wine back and forth in the bottle.)

If the wine is truly a rare one, some hosts decant, rinse the original bottle, and then pour the wine back into it for serving. This allows guests to see which great wine they are sharing. A somewhat simpler means of achieving the same end is to decant the wine and then to bring both the carafe or decanter and the emptied bottle to the table.

A wine accessory that continually shows up in gift shops is the pouring basket, which, theoretically, minimizes the disturbance of sediment in old reds. But in fact, the act of pouring wine from a basket disturbs sediment a great deal. However, these baskets cannot harm young wine.

Pouring Wine

Commonsense politeness governs the serving of wine. The host begins by pouring a small serving in his own glass to catch any stray bits of cork and to make sure the wine is sound.

When the meal is casual, the bottle is passed around the table hand to hand. On mildly formal occasions, the host circles the table once, clockwise, filling each glass. If he is in tie and tails, he moves around the table clockwise to serve the ladies; then he fills the men's glasses on the counter-clockwise return trip.

A wineglass is filled only halfway so that the air space necessary to capture the full aroma of the wine when drinking it is ensured.

Glasses for Wine

The ideal wineglass has three characteristics: It is stemmed so that warm hands do not have to be wrapped around cool wine; it is clear because color is one of the pleasures of wine; and it has a large bowl with a lip that is slightly smaller than the diameter of the bowl so that the aroma is concentrated in a generous but confined air space. (Serious students swirl wine in the glass so that its aroma volatilizes more vigorously in the head space, allowing them to smell the wine more fully and accurately.)

Though a different glass has evolved for every kind of wine, the nine-ounce all-purpose wineglass meets the basic glass requirements and is widely used for drinking any wine. The all-purpose glass can be used singly for casual meals or in clusters for formal occasions.

Time has equipped each of the major wine-growing regions of Europe

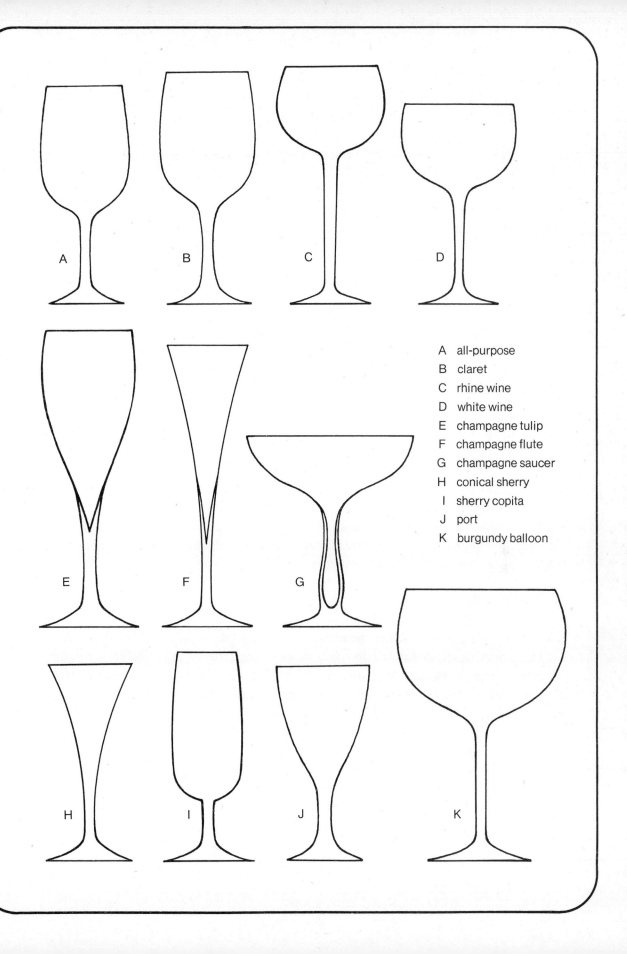

A all-purpose
B claret
C rhine wine
D white wine
E champagne tulip
F champagne flute
G champagne saucer
H conical sherry
I sherry copita
J port
K burgundy balloon

with one or more distinctive glass styles. Though these are imported into the United States, we regard them as optional grace notes. Although they may be used at informal dinners, many people reserve them for elaborate meals calling for a sequence of wines and thus for a showy display of appropriate glassware.

The traditional sherry glass is tall and shaped somewhat like a chimney. A three-ounce serving fills it halfway. Port glasses are shaped similarly, but they are more stubby.

The most identifiable glass for white wine is the one for Rhine wines; it has an almost spherical bowl set atop a long stem or, in the Mosel variation, a fancy pedestal. Glasses for white Burgundies and Bordeaux are merely scaled-down editions of red wine glasses for those regions. All three white wine glasses hold about four ounces when filled to the halfway mark.

Bordeaux and Burgundy red wine glasses hold about six ounces when they are half full. The Bordeaux is tulip-shaped; the Burgundy is balloonish.

There are three glasses for sparkling wine. The familiar one—the shallow saucer on a stem, called the coupe—lets bubbles escape too fast to be acceptable. A better design for such wine is the champagne tulip, shaped as its name suggests. A third choice is the flute, a slender cone that resembles a pilsener beer glass.

However many glasses one uses, they are arrayed on the table in order of their use. A single place setting is, right to left, sherry glass, white wine glass, red wine glass, water glass. The dessert wine glass is not included in the original setting but is brought in with the dessert. If champagne replaces the sherry or port, its glass is treated as the one it replaces. Each glass is removed as the course it accompanies comes to an end.

Storing Leftover Wine

Sometimes wine is left over at the end of a meal.

The problems that beset opened bottles (heat, light, air) are the same ones that attack full bottles, only more so and faster. Susceptibility varies by wine type. Dessert and appetizer wines keep for relatively long periods after they are opened. Tables wines keep for considerably less time, and sparkling wines go flat very quickly.

In part, the time of demise depends on whether you plan to drink the wine or to cook with it.

Sparkling wines These cannot be prevented from going flat once they are opened. If champagne is left over at the end of an evening, recork it at the earliest moment and put it into the coldest part of the refrigerator overnight.

In the morning make Champagne Orange Juice with it (see page 180) and serve them for brunch. Leftover sparkling red or pink wines are harder to dispose of, but you might use them to make a variation on the Champagne Orange Juice, substituting cranberry cocktail for the orange juice.

Sparkling wines can be used in cooking for a week or two after they have gone flat in place of a corresponding white or red table wine.

Table wines Because of sophisticated wine-making techniques, young table wines—especially the inexpensive ones—do not spoil quickly after they are opened. While it is best to drink leftover wine within a day or two, a partly full bottle can stay in drinkable condition for a week to ten days if it is tightly recapped and refrigerated. It should be all right to use in cooking for a month or more.

Red wines should be pulled out of cold storage three hours before a meal so that they can warm up. Whites and rosés may be left there until mealtime.

Buyers of jug wines (half-gallon and gallon bottles) can solve the problem of having wine left over by collecting some screw-capped fifth bottles. Wine from a new jug can be decanted into these and kept for several weeks, provided that the smaller bottles are sterilized before each filling in order to kill any vinegar bacteria. Also, the fifth bottles must be filled well into the neck, must be capped tightly, and should be stored in cool to cold temperatures.

Rare wines should not be opened until there is enough of a crowd to drink the bottle dry at one sitting. Because they are made to be elegant rather than sturdy, rare wines are likely to be of more delicate health than inexpensive wines. More importantly, they should be accorded dignity equal to their worth. If a wine is not only rare but also old, the need to finish the bottle at once is redoubled because age enfeebles wines even more than it does men.

Coating a wine with a film of oil is sometimes recommended to preserve it, but this is neither commendable nor effective. The oil gives the wine an odd taste right away and does not always stop spoilage.

Appetizer wines The key to the durability of appetizer wines is the alcohol content. The ones with alcohol contents between 14 and 17 percent are no more than modestly durable, which is to say they will stay at their best for drinking for two weeks in a cool cupboard or refrigerator; thereafter, the changes are slow but sure. Sherries with an alcohol content of 20 percent may last months without adverse effect.

61

Dessert wines   Nearly all these contain 20 percent alcohol and are very durable in an opened bottle if it is kept closed and cool between uses.

The possible exceptions are very old ports or Muscatels that have slumbered in their bottles for a decade or more. The bloom will leave these wines in a day or two, since much of their charm is in the lingering taste of fresh grapes amid all the aged flavors.

Sweet wines with only 12 percent alcohol should be treated in the same way as table wines.

62

Avocado Veal Saute, p. 126

7

Cooking with Wine

The term *wine cookery* crops up in our minds and in our talk as a thing apart from any other kind of cooking. That is too bad because cooking with wine is really no more complicated than cooking with any other winsome ingredient such as lemon juice, cinnamon, or garlic. Wine cookery does not require strange and special techniques. It simply calls for some awareness of the nice and promising source of flavor that wine truly is.

So regard wine as another pleasing ingredient, and do not be in awe of it. But *do* know that wine can bring about wondrous effects.

The main reason for using wine in cooking is for flavor—*not* for its alcoholic content (which quickly cooks away), nor for its wine aliveness nor for its magic of fermentation nor for any other mysterious effect. It is mainly for taste. That is the reason, for example, that when *haute cuisine* chefs insist on using champagne in a certain sauce, they want that unique champagne flavor, not the bubbles or the alcohol.

The flavors and aromas of wine contribute a complication, an interest, and sometimes even an exotic quality to the flavors of other ingredients in a dish, thereby enhancing and distinguishing the flavors of the other ingredients. Wine also accents the savoriness of other foods, and dry sherry tends to intensify saltiness. Finally, wine blends and brings together the flavors in a dish to give it fuller dimension—to cast a flavor-enriched aura over it and a smoothness to it.

Wine in cooking should not loudly announce itself; it should simply add a special flavor-aroma richness to the dish. Wine's role is to be an enhancer, a smoother, a helper. Only in rare cases should wine be out-and-out recognizable as an ingredient in a finished dish.

The main questions about wine cookery have simple answers.

What Happens to Wine in Cooking?

When wine is heated, three things happen.

1. The alcohol begins evaporating when it reaches its relatively low boiling point of 172.4 degrees Fahrenheit. (Water doesn't evaporate rapidly until it reaches its boiling point of 212 degrees Fahrenheit.)

2. Wine flavors change. The way they change depends on the nature of and the degree of heat applied to the wine.

If the wine is barely heated through, it can retain nearly all its flavor and even some aroma and bouquet. Two examples in this book are: finishing off a creamed chicken sauce with a sherry, pages 98 and 100, and heating a hot wine punch just to serving temperature, page 182.

The wine flavors change considerably when the wine is boiled or simmered for a length of time or is subjected to high dry heat, for then the alcohol and other volatile flavoring components of wine evaporate. The expected and hoped-for flavor effect is that of wine with a slightly bitter taste and a seeming permanence about it instead of a flighty freshness. Examples: slowly simmering beef stew meat in red wine and seasonings, page 110; basting a roasting chicken with wine and melted butter, page 104; deglazing a skillet with white wine after browning veal chops in it, page 133. (Deglazing is accomplished by adding wine or another liquid to the reduced flavor elements (brown drippings) left in a skillet or roasting pan after browning in order to loosen and dissolve the drippings. The resulting reduced liquid, blended with flavoring elements, is used in or as a sauce.)

The flavors of dessert wines and brandies change *and* take on a new taste when they are flamed. First, they lose the flavors of their volatile parts. Then the sugar contents (of the fortified wine or brandy) caramelize and add a small nuance of burnt-sugar taste. Examples: brandy-flaming the sugar-butter-citrus syrup for dessert crêpes, page 158; flaming a little brandy in the drippings resulting from browning chicken breasts and then completing a sauce using the remainder of the burned brandy as a base, page 96.

3. The wine reduces in quantity and concentrates in flavor. This occurs most obviously when cooked over high and direct heat and is known in culinary terminology as "reducing" the wine (or other liquid)—that is, cooking it so quickly that much of the liquid evaporates and the remaining flavors intensify.

How Is Wine Used in Cooking?

We have already stressed the use of wine in cooking

1. *As a source of flavor.* When you add wine to your cooking, you do not add just one flavor (as you do when you incorporate, say, mace into your baking). You add the possibility of many flavors—as many flavors as there are kinds of wine (sherry, port, fruity white wine, mellow red wine, and so forth) *and* the several flavors within one wine (sweet and tart and spicy, for example).

All the following reasons for using wine here are extensions on the use of wine as flavor—that is, it is still added chiefly for this reason.

2. *As part of a simmering or poaching liquid.* Wine may be used as part of the broth for simmering a chicken, as part of the court bouillon for poaching a fish, as part of the simmering juice for braising stew meat or a Swiss steak, as part of the syrup for poaching fresh fruits.

3. *As a baste.* Wine may be part of a basting mixture for barbecuing and

for roasting meats, fish, and poultry. Or it may be part of a basting glaze for cookies, pies, breads, and other baked products.

4. *As an addition to a sauce.* Wine may be the main constituent of a sauce, or it may be used to finish a sauce.

When wine is the main constituent of a sauce, it is added generously and is then reduced. Usually, this is done on one of two occasions. First, you may cook down the wine-seasoned liquid left from simmering or poaching and use that reduced liquid as part of a sauce. (Example: Sole Marguery, page 84.) Second, you may deglaze a skillet or roasting pan with wine and use that reduced wine blended with the drippings as part of a sauce or as the sauce. (Example: Veal Roast with White Wine, page 135.)

When wine is used to finish a sauce, you add a smaller amount of wine and you cook it very little or not at all. In this instance, wine simply gives a sauce its final, closing, rounded seasoning and consistency.

To finish a cooked sauce, you add wine at the very end of cooking—sometimes even after the sauce has been removed from the heat—because you do not want to cook away the volatile qualities of wine. To finish uncooked or cooled sauces, you add a very small amount of wine at the end of preparation; for example, you may whip a tablespoon of brandy into the whipped cream for your mincemeat pie.

It is especially important to use a light hand when adding wine as a finish because there is no chance for the alcohol to escape and you don't want to serve a sauce tasting of alcohol.

5. *As a direct saucing or seasoning.* You may add wine directly to foods to sauce or spice them—and that is all you do. For example, you may pour wine over sliced fresh fruits or a compote of fruits (as in Strawberries and Port, page 153) or ladle it over ice cream, sherbet, or custard.

6. *As a tenderizer.* Wine has a tenderizing effect on meats and poultry when used as part of a marinade and for a relatively long time (two to three days for pot roast or rabbit; at least three hours for chicken pieces, small chops, and other small cuts). Wine marinating usually contributes some wine flavoring.

7. *As an addition of liquid content.*

8. *As an addition of acid content and acid action.* Because of its acid content, wine may be used in cooking in the same way as lemon juice and vinegar. Like those two ingredients, wine may add a flavor sharpness. Also, the especially high acid wines call for some caution in using them with ingredients that curdle easily such as milk, cream, and eggs. A good cook's precaution is simply to use relatively small amounts of high-acid wine in combination with such touchy ingredients and to add the wine very gradually.

In fish cookery wine distinguishes the delicate flavors of fish and, at the same time, neutralizes any oily, fishy flavor and aroma.

9. *As a flaming agent.* The flaming of wines in cooking is partly for flavor and partly—when done at serving time—for flair. Only fortified wines and brandy have an alcohol content high enough to ignite easily. Table wines do not flame successfully.

Certainly, you may use more than one of these ways or reasons for wine cookery in the preparation of a single dish. For example, a good cook might use wine as part of the poaching liquid for a fish and then make a wine-seasoned sauce from the reduced liquid (Dilled Sole in White Wine, page 83). Or she may simmer stew meat in red wine and other seasonings, let those juices become the stew sauce, and, just before serving, finish the sauce with a tablespoon or so of the red wine to give a final, subtle wine overtone (Semi-Classical Beef Burgundy, page 110). This technique is an excellent way to give a dish the flavor benefits of both long-cooked wine and wine almost as pure and as complete as when poured straight from the bottle.

What Wines Should Be Used in Cooking?

Though all kinds of wine cook much the same, all wines certainly do not contribute the same flavors to food. Wines differ in their flavor effects in cooking just as they differ in flavor when drunk from a glass (their essential wine types)—sweet, dry, white, red, fortified, low alcohol. So you select the wine for your cooking according to the flavors it provides and the nature of what is being cooked.

A general rule is to use the same type of wine in cooking a dish as you would drink with the dish. For example, a nice, light, refreshing white wine is wonderfully pleasing with a chilled chicken salad, so the same wine would be right to use in seasoning the salad's dressing. Or, since a sturdy beef stew calls for a hearty red wine as the best companion, the same hearty red would be an appropriate ingredient in the stew itself.

In cooking, one dry white table wine is usually interchangeable with another, and the same is true of dry reds, because the cooking process changes wine enough so that small differences are not apparent. Thus, when a recipe calls for a dry white wine, you can probably use a dry sauterne, Chablis, or Rhine wine with success, or if it calls for a dry red wine, you can use a Burgundy or a claret. But there are occasions when subtlety is important. For example, an especially elegant beef dish may call for a soft Pinot Noir as a finish; if you used a more tart Cabernet Sauvignon, all the smooth, round subtleties leading to the perfect wine finish might be contradicted.

Sometimes the essential wine type to go into a dish is different from the wine to be drunk with it. You might use a little brandy to finish a light cream sauce for veal chops, yet you would certainly not drink brandy with the veal. Or you might add a few spoonfuls of sherry to your chicken à la king sauce, but the pleasant wine to drink with the dish is a nice dry white—not sherry.

The question is often raised as to what quality of wine to use in cooking. The simple answer is to use a sound wine of a quality appropriate to the dish, which will often be the wine you are serving with the meal. If you are cooking a casual supper of spaghetti and a husky sausage–garlic tomato sauce, a generous amount of an uncomplicated, hearty red is fine to add to the sauce and to drink with the meal. If you are preparing delicate medallions of veal cloaked with a creamy wine sauce, you should finish the sauce with a small measure of fine wine, just as fine a wine as you would want to drink with so luxurious a dish. It is logical that if you are using a small amount of wine to finish a sauce, you can comfortably and reasonably use a more elegant wine than you could were you putting a large amount of wine into a long-cooked dish in which the wine flavor is bound to recede and change considerably.

Many supermarkets and delicatessens carry bottles labeled "cooking wine." Do not be tempted to buy them, as the so-called wine is not for drinking. If wine is not fine enough to drink, it is not fine enough to use as one ingredient among your other carefully chosen ingredients.

Some people believe that when you do not have a dry white wine handy, you may substitute dry vermouth as an ingredient. The idea is sound as a general principle, but it is safer left to experienced wine cooks than to novices. Dry vermouth does not invariably interchange with dry white wine. Sometimes the vermouth gives too pronounced a flavor; sometimes it needs dilution by about one-third water; sometimes it needs the addition of lemon or lime juice to give the fruity effect that the designated wine would have had. In other words, dry vermouth can be a reasonable backup for a dry white wine in cooking, but it is not ideal.

8

Appetizers

The ideal appetizer awakens hunger and appeases it at the same time—but only slightly, for there is still a meal to come. Intense flavors, such as those of liver, chutney, and onion, will stir hunger and also discourage over-indulgence; thus, classic hors d'oeuvres and first courses often feature these and other highly flavorful foods.

Likewise, the foremost appetizer wine is dry sherry, with its heightened flavor that stems from its alcoholic content and long aging in warm cellars. As a further assist to willpower, sherry glasses hold no more than three ounces. The driest champagnes join sherry as being a fine wine to start a meal, again because their flavors are intense enough to make one glass satisfying.

The recipes and wine recommendations in this chapter adhere to tradition for the most part, but there are exceptions. In earlier times, the appetizer was the prelude to a meal of many courses—then it was essential to go light with the appetizer and accompanying wine. But contemporary meals seldom run to more than three or four courses, so that the first course can play a bigger role, whether it is eaten standing as an hors d'oeuvre or seated as a formal first course. For this reason we sometimes recommend a white wine or a less-than-dry sparkling one as the accompanying beverage.

You will know whether you want people to go heavy at the beginning of the meal or whether you want them to arrive at the main course still wearing a lean-and-hungry look.

Chutney Cheese Pâté

This is a dish of contrasts—sharp chutney against soft cheese, crispy cracker against smooth pâté. The buttery flavor of sherry brings a harmony to the whole, as well as serving to moisten the pâté.

6 ounces soft cream cheese
¼ pound (about 1 cup) shredded sharp natural Cheddar cheese
About 2 tablespoons dry sherry
About ¾ teaspoon curry powder
About ¼ teaspoon salt
Dash of Tabasco

½ cup finely chopped mango Chutney
3 to 4 green onions, with part of green tops, minced
Crisp sesame wafers or wheat crackers

Beat together cream cheese, Cheddar cheese, sherry, curry powder, salt, and Tabasco until almost smooth. Spread on a serving platter, shaping a layer about ½ inch thick; leave room around the edge for crackers. Chill until firm.

At serving time, spread chutney over top of mixture and sprinkle with onion. Surround with crackers, and provide a knife for spreading. 6 to 8 servings.

72

BASIC WINE CHOICE: Pale dry sherry

Because this pâté represents such a delicate balance of flavors and textures, it is worth going to some trouble to find a sherry that is indeed pale and dry. We have taken particular pleasure in Concannon's Prelude, Almaden's Fino, and Gallo's Old Decanter Pale Dry.

For a group of eight, we think a brut champagne is a joyous and sensible idea.

Sherry-broiled Shrimp

When you serve these shrimp as stand-up finger food, the guests pick the shrimp up and handle them by the tail. When you serve the shrimp as a sit-down first course, the guests may use fingers or forks. In either case, provide plenty of napkins.

1½ pounds large raw shrimp (8- to 15-per-pound size)
½ cup olive oil
¼ cup dry sherry
2 large cloves garlic, minced or mashed
¼ cup finely chopped fresh parsley

About ¾ teaspoon salt
About ½ teaspoon freshly ground black pepper
¼ teaspoon crumbled dried thyme
About ⅛ teaspoon crushed dried hot red peppers

Shell and devein shrimp, leaving tail shells on.

Combine remaining ingredients in a bowl, add shrimp, and allow to stand at room temperature for 1 hour (or 2 hours or more in refrigerator); turn occasionally.

Preheat broiler. Arrange shrimp in marinade in a single layer in a shallow broiling pan. Broil about 6 inches from heat *just* until shrimp turn pink and lose translucence, about 4 minutes on each side. Serve hot with marinade spooned over. 6 servings.

73

BASIC WINE CHOICE: Dry or medium sherry

Any dry or medium sherry will offset the weight of olive oil and garlic in this appetizer. Good examples are Louis M. Martini's Dry Sherry and Taylor's Pale Dry Sherry.

Sherry Appetizer Bouillon

Because this soup cooks for a long time over low heat, all alcohol vanishes, leaving only the heightened flavor of sherry that merges smoothly with the bouillon.

If this is sipped directly from cups, a sherry as a beverage is too much. However, if the soup is spooned from bowls, a cooled dry sherry would go with it agreeably.

2 cans (10½ ounces each) condensed beef broth, undiluted	**2 bouillon cans dry sherry**
	6 thin lime slices

Combine broth and sherry in a saucepan. Place over low heat (below simmering), uncovered, for 1 hour. Strain through a linen napkin or a very fine sieve to remove thin film. Reheat if necessary.

Place a lime slice in each of 6 soup cups. Pour broth over and serve. 6 servings.

74

Sherried Oranges

If you wish, garnish these sherried oranges with a few washed green leaves or with fresh rosemary sprigs.

6 oranges	**1½ teaspoons crumbled dried**
¾ cup dry sherry	**rosemary**
Salt to taste	

Peel oranges, removing and discarding all membrane; slice thinly. Arrange in a shallow glass serving bowl or in individual shallow dishes. Sprinkle with sherry, a few grains of salt, and rosemary. Chill thoroughly and serve. 6 servings.

BASIC WINE CHOICE: Dry sherry

Because of the oranges, this dish calls not for the driest of dry sherries but rather for one that is more medium-dry, such as Guild's Old Ceremony Dry, Weibel's Dry Wit, and Souverain's Los Amigos Dry Sack.

Molded Pâté with Wine Aspic

Wine in the aspic serves as a bridge between the buttery smoothness of the pâté and the refreshing qualities of the drinking wine. Guests spread the pâté on small slices of caraway-seeded rye bread or toast and then top each one with a forkful of aspic and a sprig of watercress.

1 pound chicken livers	⅛ teaspoon ground cloves
1 cup soft butter	¹⁄₁₆ teaspoon cayenne
¼ cup minced green onions, white part only	Rye bread (or toast) with caraway seeds, sliced thin and buttered
1½ teaspoons dry mustard	Wine Aspic (recipe follows)
½ teaspoon ground nutmeg	Watercress sprigs
About ¼ teaspoon salt	

Place livers in a saucepan with water to cover; heat to boiling. Reduce heat and simmer for 30 minutes, or until very tender. Allow livers to cool slightly in water, then drain well.

Place livers and butter in blender container and whirl at medium speed until mixture is very smooth. Stir in onions, mustard, nutmeg, salt, cloves, and cayenne.

Spread mixture in a lightly oiled, shallow 3-cup mold; press gently to remove any air bubbles. Cover and chill until firm.

About 30 minutes before serving time, dip mold in warm water for a few moments to loosen pâté, then turn out on serving platter. At serving time, surround with bread or toast, aspic dice, and watercress. About 12 servings.

Wine Aspic

1 teaspoon unflavored gelatin	⅔ cup canned condensed beef consommé, undiluted
⅔ cup dry white wine	

Sprinkle gelatin into wine in a saucepan and allow to soften. Add beef consommé; stir over low heat until gelatin is dissolved. Pour into an 8-inch square pan and chill until set. Cut into about ¼-inch dices and lift out.

BASIC WINE CHOICE: Fruity white

Sherry is by no means inevitable as the beginning beverage of a dinner. What this dish needs is a wine that will cut through the creamy richness of a liver pâté, offering what might be called a cleansing relief. Although sherry could do the job, a dry spicy Gewürztraminer will do even better; Louis Martini's, in particular, mates well with this pâté. The combination is appropriate enough: Both the pâté and Gewürztraminer have their origins in Alsace, where they have been paired for more than a century.

Sherry Shellfish Soup

Though crab and sherry are full-flavored ingredients, this soup is truly delicate in character. It may be served in small portions before a complete dinner for six or ladled out with a generous hand as the major part of a supper. Slender bread sticks go well with it.

⅔ cup dry sherry
½ pound (about 1 cup) flaked crab meat
3½ cups regular-strength chicken broth
2 teaspoons very finely grated onion
2 teaspoons grated fresh lemon peel

2 teaspoons fresh lemon juice
¾ teaspoon ground mace
⅔ cup heavy cream, divided
3 tablespoons finely chopped celery leaves
Cayenne

Pour sherry over crab in a bowl, and let stand for 30 minutes. In a saucepan, slowly heat broth with onion, lemon peel, lemon juice, and mace. Add crab, sherry, and 4 tablespoons of the cream; slowly heat through, but do not boil.

Softly whip remaining cream. Ladle soup into 6 small warmed serving bowls or pots. Top each serving with a sprinkling of celery leaves, a spoonful of whipped cream, and a dash of cayenne. 6 servings.

BASIC WINE CHOICE: Light white

A delicate white wine is the best accompaniment to this dish. Almost any Chablis mates gracefully. Avoid the flowery wines—Johannisberg Riesling, Gewürztraminer, and their kin, as they tend to overpower the soup.

Chilled Plum Pot

This may be served as a first course or as a dessert soup. Either way, there is enough wine in it so that you will not want to drink wine with it. Accompany the first-course soup with lightly salted wafer crackers, the dessert soup with unsweetened wafer cookies.

1 can (1 pound 14 ounces) purple plums in heavy syrup	¼ teaspoon ground cinnamon
¾ cup dry white wine	Pinch of salt
2 tablespoon fresh lemon juice	6 thin lemon slices

Remove pits from plums. Put plums with syrup into blender container with wine, lemon juice, cinnamon, and salt, and whirl at medium speed until smooth. Chill thoroughly. Stir well and serve in chilled bowls or soup cups. Garnish each serving with a slice of lemon. 6 servings.

9

Fish and Shellfish

Cooking fish in wine serves several related purposes.

When it is used as a poaching liquid for delicately flavored fish, wine sustains the flavor of the fish rather than thinning it, as water does.

When used as a marinade, wine helps to cook fish just a bit. Thus, the cooking time over heat is shortened so that a moister fish arrives on the serving plate. (Cooks who are familiar with the Swedish salmon dish Gravlax or the Mexican Ceviche know that fish can be cooked using no heat at all, but only natural fruit acids. Wine has enough fruit acid to make a gentle start in the same direction.)

The same tart qualities of wine tend to counter fish oils. This means that a tart wine makes a fish taste less fishy in much the same way a lemon does, although to a far lesser degree because no wine is quite as tart as lemon. Wine serves this purpose whether used as a marinade, a poaching liquid, or a baste.

Wine and fish at the table are the stuff of durable memories. A rich Chardonnay with lobster and drawn butter; a fresh Johannisberg Riesling with cold cracked crab; a deft, dry Pinot Blanc with sole—all have the power to launch thoughts of next time even before you get up from the table. (Contrarily, Grey Riesling and scallops lead to a vow not to make the pairing again because each makes the other taste like cod liver oil.)

Generalities about the right and wrong wines are very hard to make in the case of fish and shellfish. If there is a single rule, it is this: Light, fresh wines go with delicately flavored, flaky textured fish, such as sole (and also clams); the heavier and richer the seafood becomes, the richer and fuller the wine must be to avoid an oily taste in both. The recipes and recommendations in this chapter follow the rule.

Dry wines are easier than sweet, and young ones easier than old, when being mated with fish and shellfish, though as usual there are exceptions in specific instances.

Red wine and fish and shellfish can be made to go together if spice gives added strength to the fish; without vehement spicing, some fish flavors tend to be too delicate. The classic good example is a hearty tomato sauce of the sort used for bouillabaisse or cioppino.

A Many-Fish White-Wine Soup

This soup celebrates the freshness of the seafood that goes into it by keeping those tastes uncluttered and pure. The wine and fresh vegetables provide a simplified background for showing off the good seafood.

This is a full-meal soup, requiring no more accompaniment than toasted French bread and wine, and perhaps a green salad and cheese afterward. If you wish, brush the bread with garlic and olive oil or butter before toasting.

1 very large onion, finely chopped
2 carrots, finely chopped
¼ cup olive oil
2 bottles (8 ounces each) clam juice
2 cups dry white wine
4 cloves garlic, minced or mashed
⅓ cup finely chopped fresh parsley
1 bay leaf
½ teaspoon crumbled dried thyme
¼ teaspoon freshly ground black pepper

⅛ teaspoon sugar
Generous dash of Tabasco
1½ dozens hardshell clams in shells, scrubbed
1 can (1 pound) peeled tomatoes, drained, seeded, and chopped
1½ pounds fillets of lean white fish—such as red snapper or other rockfish, bass, or halibut—cut into 2-inch squares
1 pound medium shrimp, shelled and deveined
Salt to taste
Finely chopped fresh parsley

80

In a large kettle, sauté the onion and carrots in oil until limp. Add clam juice, wine, garlic, ⅓ cup parsley, bay leaf, thyme, pepper, sugar, and Tabasco; heat to boiling. Reduce heat and simmer, uncovered, for 5 minutes. Add clams, and simmer for 5 more minutes. Add tomatoes and fish, and simmer for 2 more minutes. Add shrimp, and simmer for 3 more minutes, or until shrimp are pink and clams are open. Add salt, if necessary.

Ladle into shallow soup plates. Sprinkle each serving with a very small amount of chopped parsley. 6 servings.

BASIC WINE CHOICE: Light white

The many flavorful ingredients of this soup produce an amazingly gentle effect. Therefore, the wine to drink should be unobtrusive, the equivalent of an obbligato in music. Chablis goes well, particularly the one from The Christian Brothers. Among varietals, a Sylvaner or Traminer are fine choices.

Baked Fish with Baste of Wine and Butter

In this recipe, wine serves as a baste—a constant one—for the baking fish.

A piece of a whole large fish may be substituted for the fillets in this recipe; simply increase the baking time until the fish flakes.

Thick ripe tomato slices provide the right salad.

½ cup butter	2 pounds fillets of red
1 cup minced green onions, with	snapper or other rockfish,
part of green tops	bass, or steelhead
2 teaspoons fresh lemon juice	Salt and freshly ground black
¾ cup dry white wine, divided	pepper to taste

Preheat oven to moderate (350°).

In a skillet, heat butter over medium-high heat until it foams and browns. Add onion, and sauté until limp. Stir in lemon juice and wine, reserving 2 tablespoons of the wine for later use.

Wipe fish dry with a damp cloth. Season surfaces generously with salt and pepper. Place in a single layer in an oiled shallow baking dish. Pour onion mixture over. Bake just until thickest part of fish flakes with a fork about 20 minutes; baste occasionally with pan juices.

Lift fish to serving plates or platter. Stir remaining wine into pan juices, and spoon over fish. 4 servings.

BASIC WINE CHOICE: Light white

Red snapper, rockfish, and bass belong to the delicately flavored, flaky textured school of fish, and so go well with Chablis, Sylvaner, and other delicately flavored wines. This does not rule out Johannisberg Riesling or dry Chenin Blanc for those who prefer more weight to their wines. (As a committee of two we found ourselves deadlocked on the question of Johannisberg but agreed on Chablis.)

Snapper Yucatan

This dish comes from Merida, Yucatan, the heart of the old Mayan culture and cuisine. There, the family-managed Las Palomas restaurant presents it executed according to the ancestral Yucatecan recipe. The spicing is simple and fresh. The wine ingredient is a dry white Mexican one, but a California white does just as well in touching the fish with its flavor. Manager Mario Peña responds to praise quietly: "After all, you come three thousand miles here. I want to give you something special." He does.

Serve the fish in scooped dinner plates or shallow soup bowls and accompany with spoons so that eaters won't miss the wine sauce.

2 pounds fillets of red snapper or other rockfish
¼ cup dry white wine
⅓ cup olive oil
1 very large tomato, peeled, seeded, and finely chopped
¼ cup finely chopped fresh parsley
1 tablespoon grated onion
1 large clove garlic, minced or mashed
1 tablespoon fresh lime juice

¾ teaspoon salt
½ teaspoon crumbled dried oregano
About ¼ teaspoon crushed dried hot red peppers (more if you want a hotter sauce)
¼ teaspoon freshly ground black pepper
⅛ teaspoon sugar
4 thin lime slices
4 parsley sprigs

Preheat oven to moderate (350°).

Wipe fish dry with a damp cloth. Arrange close together in a single layer in an oiled shallow baking dish. Sprinkle with wine. With a fork, combine the remaining ingredients except lime slices and parsley sprigs; mix well and spoon over fish.

Bake just until thickest part of fish flakes with a fork, about 20 minutes. Serve with all baking juices ladled over, and garnish each serving with a lime slice and parsley sprig. 4 servings.

BASIC WINE CHOICE: Full, dry white

We recommend Chardonnay in several instances as a rich wine to go with rich dishes. In this case, nothing less than the powerful flavor of a Chardonnay can counter the distinctly peppery flavor of Mexico.

Dilled Sole in White Wine

Here, Trader Vic shares his idea for Sole Menehune. As the wine poaches into the fish, it tenderizes and flavors. The wine alone, however, would be too sharp a sauce for the subtle fish, which is the reason that the mellowing chicken broth is added.

Provide spoons as well as forks for your guests so that they can enjoy the sauce. Consider fresh peas as a vegetable and thin-sliced fresh tomatoes as a salad.

The same treatment works very well for trout. Substitute four whole cleaned trout, each about one-half pound, for the sole, and poach in wine broth just until they begin to flake. Otherwise, follow the recipe.

4 fillets of sole or flounder, about 1¼ to 1½ pounds total	1 tablespoon minced green onions, white part only
Salt and freshly ground black pepper to taste	1 tablespoon butter
1½ cups dry white wine	About ½ teaspoon dried dillweed
½ cup chicken broth	1 cup heavy cream

Preheat oven to warm (200°).

Wipe fish dry with a damp cloth, and season lightly with salt and pepper. Combine wine, broth, and onion in a large heavy skillet; heat to bubbling. Add fish, arranging in a single layer; cook, uncovered, just until liquid returns to bubbling and fish surfaces turn white (while you make the sauce, the fish will continue to cook in the oven until it barely flakes with a fork). With a slotted spatula, lift fish, drain it well, and place it on warmed serving plates or platter; place in oven.

Cook liquid in skillet over high heat until reduced to about ¾ cup. Add butter, dill, and cream; cook over high heat, stirring, until liquid is reduced to consistency of thick cream and is very slightly golden. Correct seasoning, if necessary, and pour over fish. 4 servings.

BASIC WINE CHOICE: Light white

In contrast to Sole Marguery, Sole Menehune focuses attention on the fish itself. The Chablis or Sylvaner produced by Beaulieu Vineyard makes an adroit companion to this dish.

Sole Marguery

This dish from Jack's restaurant in San Francisco is a justly renowned classic and a very rich meal.

In the preparation you will use two basic wine cookery techniques: poaching in wine (wine and stock make the simple court bouillon for poaching), and reducing wine (wine is cooked down and concentrated before being made a part of the sauce).

8 small fillets of sole or flounder, about 2 pounds total
Salt and freshly ground black pepper to taste
3 tablespoons minced shallots or ¼ cup minced green onions, white part only, and ½ small clove garlic, minced or mashed
¼ pound fresh mushrooms, thinly sliced

12 Dungeness crab legs, or large pieces of other crab, about 4 ounces total
3 to 4 ounces tiny shelled cooked shrimp
1 cup dry white wine
1 cup fish stock or water
1 cup heavy cream
¼ cup Hollandaise Sauce (recipe follows)

84

Preheat oven to moderate (350°).

Wipe fillets dry with a damp cloth, season lightly with salt and pepper, and fold each in half, crosswise. Arrange in a single layer in an oiled baking dish. Sprinkle with shallots, mushrooms, crab, and shrimp; add wine and stock. Bake just until fish flakes with a fork, about 15 minutes.

Carefully pour off juices into a wide saucepan (or remove fish, mushrooms, crab, and shrimp to a clean, buttered broiling–serving platter). Add cream to baking juices, and cook over high heat, stirring, until reduced to the consistency of thick cream. Remove from heat and stir in Hollandaise. Pour sauce over fish and slip dish under broiler, about 6 inches from heat, until glazed with brown. 4 servings.

Hollandaise Sauce

3 egg yolks
2 tablespoons fresh lemon
   juice
¼ teaspoon salt

Pinch of cayenne
½ cup butter
½ teaspoon Dijon-style mustard

Put first 4 ingredients into blender container. Heat butter in saucepan until it bubbles; do not brown. Turn blender on high speed, and immediately pour hot butter in a steady stream through small opening in blender's cover. Add mustard, and continue whirling blender for about 15 seconds, or until mixture is blended. Makes ¾ to 1 cup sauce.

NOTE: To reheat remaining unused portion of Hollandaise for later use, place in top part of double boiler over hot (not boiling) water; stir until smooth and warm.

BASIC WINE CHOICE: Fruity white

Here is an example of the sauce determining which wine to serve. What goes very well with the creamy Marguery is a dry Chenin Blanc or something closely kindred. Louis M. Martini's Dry Chenin Blanc and Charles Krug's White Pinot (also made from Chenin Blanc grapes, in spite of its muddled name) are recommended, while Pinot Blancs head our list of close, acceptable kin.

85

Fillets, Wisconsin au Gratin

In this recipe you may use white fish fillets from any waters—salt or fresh—but it is especially designed for the fish from freshwater lakes and rivers.

A vegetable suggestion: hot fresh spinach.

2 pounds fillets of fresh fish (such as whitefish, pike, trout, perch, bass, or muskellunge)	**2½ tablespoons fresh lemon juice**
	1½ tablespoons dry sherry
	1 cup heavy cream
Salt and freshly ground black pepper to taste	**About 1 cup shredded sharp natural Cheddar cheese**

Preheat oven to moderate (350°).

Wipe fish dry with damp cloth, and season generously with salt and pepper. Arrange in bottom of an oiled shallow baking dish (fish layer should be about ¾ inch thick). Sprinkle with lemon juice and sherry. Pour cream over. Sprinkle with cheese.

Bake just until fish flakes with a fork, about 20 minutes. Spoon the sauce over fish as you serve. 4 servings.

86

BASIC WINE CHOICE: Light white

This dish calls for a truly tart wine, such as Mirassou's White Burgundy.

Fresh Salmon Baked in Wine Cream

Because salmon is a rich fish, it needs a tart contrast—in a side dish or a sauce or, at the very least, a bit of lemon squeezed over it. In this recipe, wine in the sauce acts as the tart factor; it also contributes flavor and tenderizes slightly.

For a vegetable salad, serve thinly sliced cucumbers and tomatoes sprinkled lightly with dillweed or fresh basil.

4 pieces salmon fillets, each about ½ pound Salt, divided 1¼ cups heavy cream	2 tablespoons minced green onions, white part only ¼ cup dry white wine

Preheat oven to hot (400°).

Wipe fish dry with a damp cloth; sprinkle lightly with salt. Arrange fillets in a single layer, slightly apart, in an oiled shallow baking dish.

With a fork, mix cream, onion, and ½ teaspoon salt; gradually beat in the wine. Pour over fish. Bake just until fish flakes with a fork, about 20 minutes. Spoon cream sauce over fish as you serve. 4 servings.

87

BASIC WINE CHOICE: Full dry white

Chardonnay is the ticket—above all, a Chardonnay that has been aged in French oak barrels to enhance its staying power and richness of flavor. The principal candidates are the Chardonnays from Beaulieu, Heitz, Charles Krug, and Robert Mondavi. Those who have access to rarer wines might wish to savor the Chardonnays from Chalone, Hanzell, Freemark Abbey, and Stony Hill. Any Chardonnay is a better idea than no Chardonnay at all.

Oysters Chablis

Here, oysters are cloaked in a sauce reduced from the juices that poach them, and then slipped under the broiler to acquire a glaze. The wine lends pungency to an otherwise soft set of flavors. The delicate, yet satisfying, dish can also be served as a first course for six.

1½ cups dry white wine	3 tablespoons peeled, seeded, and chopped tomato
½ cup chicken broth	
2 tablespoons minced green onions, white part only	2 tablespoons snipped fresh chives
2 jars (10 ounces each) Eastern or small Pacific oysters, rinsed and drained	2 tablespoons minced fresh parsley
1 tablespoon butter	Salt and freshly ground black pepper to taste
1 cup heavy cream, divided	

In a large heavy skillet, heat wine and broth with onions until simmering. Add oysters, and simmer until edges curl, about 3 minutes. With a slotted spoon, remove oysters. Cook liquid in pan over high heat until reduced to about ¾ cup; strain, and return to pan. Add butter, ⅔ cup of the cream, and the tomato; cook over high heat, stirring, until liquid is reduced to consistency of thick cream and is slightly golden. Stir in chives and parsley. Season sauce with salt and pepper, and fold in oysters.

Preheat broiler. Divide mixture among oiled shallow baking dishes, one for each serving. Whip remaining cream, and spread over oysters. Slip dishes under broiler, about 5 inches from heat, until cream glazes to a deep brown. 3 servings.

BASIC WINE CHOICE: Full dry white

One of the great poetic thoughts about oysters is that their flavor recalls to a man the origins of life on earth; oysters are, in the truest sense, elemental. So it is that oysters on the half shell traditionally require dry, earthy wines that smack of the earth.

This dish does not tamper with that tradition. Chardonnays, Pinot Blancs, genuinely dry Chenin Blancs, and genuinely dry Chablis all assist the oysters in evoking elemental earth; a year or two of bottle age helps the effect. Brut champagne is a good choice, too, because the yeasts that make the bubbles also impart an earthy quality to the wine. Korbel makes the point well.

88

Lobster Newburg

Here is a memorable exception to the rule that you drink with a dish the same wine you cook into it. To be rich, Newburg sauce needs sherry, but a white wine is far better for drinking.

You can prepare the sauce ahead of time. Make it and then cool it while stirring occasionally; cover and chill. Reheat the sauce in the top of a double boiler over hot (not boiling) water, stirring.

The lobster meat in a Newburg may be from boiled lobster tails (slice the meat crosswise about ⅛ inch thick) or pieces of spiny lobster meat or canned lobster meat (drain well and break into large pieces).

You can change the recipe to shrimp or crab Newburg simply by substituting corresponding amounts of these shellfish for the lobster meat.

A nice salad to have after the Newburg is butter or Boston lettuce and fresh orange slices with a light oil, lemon juice, and vinegar dressing.

1 **cup dairy half-and-half (light cream)**
2 **egg yolks**
¼ **teaspoon salt**
⅓ **cup dry or medium-dry sherry**
3 **tablespoons butter**
¼ **teaspoon freshly ground black pepper**
⅛ **teaspoon paprika**
Generous dash of Tabasco
⅔ **pound lobster meat, cooked**
Warm buttered toast points, or toast cups or patty shells
Watercress sprigs

Scald half-and-half in a saucepan.

In a bowl, slightly beat egg yolks with salt. Whisking or beating constantly, gradually add sherry. Continue whisking, and gradually add hot half-and-half. Return mixture to saucepan and cook over low heat, stirring constantly, just until it coats a silver spoon and is slightly thickened, about 8 minutes; do not allow to boil.

Melt butter in a skillet, and stir in pepper, paprika, and Tabasco. Add lobster meat and, over low heat, turn just to coat with butter and heat through. Pour sherry sauce over lobster; gently turn and heat through. Add salt if necessary. Serve over toast points, or in toast cups or patty shells, and garnish generously with watercress. 3 servings.

BASIC WINE CHOICE: Full dry white

Chardonnay and Pinot Blanc go very well with lobster whether the meat is served alone or in a sauce such as this one. They are rich wines, suited to rich meats. Chardonnay is also a very dry wine and, to some people, a bit daunting. If you prefer a soft white, you may find Souverain's Pineau or Robert Mondavi's Fumé Blanc a worthy companion to the buttery blessings of this Newburg.

Crab au Gratin

Here is a case when wine serves as both the base of the sauce and the finishing ingredient. The wine is cooked so little that it does not change form markedly, which allows it to serve well in both capacities.

You can assemble this casserole a few hours ahead of time, chill it, and then top it with crumbs and bake in time to serve. If the casserole is chilled, increase baking time accordingly.

Serve alongside or over hot steamed rice.

½ **pound fresh mushrooms, thinly**
   sliced
2 **tablespoons minced green**
   onions, white part only
¼ **cup butter**
Wine Béchamel Sauce (recipe
   follows)

1½ **pounds (about 3 cups) large**
    pieces of frozen, thawed
    king crab or other crab
3 **cups fine soft bread crumbs**
6 **tablespoons melted butter**

Preheat oven to moderate (350°).

In a large skillet, sauté mushrooms and onions in the ¼ cup butter over medium–high heat until tender. Fold into Wine Béchamel Sauce along with crab. Turn into a 2½-quart oiled shallow baking dish. Toss bread crumbs with the 6 tablespoons melted butter, and sprinkle over top.

Bake, uncovered, for about 30 minutes, or until bubbling and heated through. If crumbs are not browned, slip casserole under broiler until crumbs are a rich golden brown. 6 servings.

Wine Béchamel Sauce

6 tablespoons butter
6 tablespoons flour
¾ teaspoon salt
1¾ cups milk
¼ cup heavy cream
1 cup dry white wine
1¼ teaspoons Worcestershire
sauce
Dash of Tabasco

½ teaspoon freshly ground
black pepper
⅛ teaspoon monosodium
glutamate
2 tablespoons finely chopped
fresh parsley
1 large clove garlic, minced
or mashed

In a saucepan over medium heat, melt butter; add flour and salt and stir to make a smooth paste. Remove from heat, and gradually whisk in milk and cream.

Return to heat; cook and whisk until sauce is smooth and thickened. Remove from heat, and gradually whisk in wine, Worcestershire, Tabasco, pepper, monosodium glutamate, parsley, and garlic.

BASIC WINE CHOICE: Fruity white

The béchamel sauce, the butter, the mushrooms—these ingredients constitute an indulgence that can be only redoubled with a wine of soft and rounded charms. At the inexpensive end of the scale, a Rhine wine may be the choice. Among varietals, Chenin Blanc, Fumé Blanc, and Johannisberg Riesling show an appropriate lack of hard edges.

Coquilles St. Jacques à la Parisienne

The Parisienne style of scallops in the shell has scallops and mushrooms being poached in white wine and finished in a white wine sauce. Though traditional in France as a first course, Coquilles St. Jacques is often too rich in that position for American tastes. Here it is presented as a main course for luncheon or supper; as a first course, it will serve six.

Do not be concerned that you might be "watering down" the sauce by adding water to the poaching liquid. All the water will boil off as you reduce the liquid nearly to its essence for the sauce.

You can prepare the recipe ahead of time up to the point of baking, chill, and then heat in time to serve.

1½ cups dry white wine	1½ pounds fresh sea scallops
¾ teaspoon salt	¾ pound fresh mushrooms, thinly sliced
1/16 teaspoon freshly ground black pepper	Sauce Parisienne (recipe follows)
1 small bay leaf	⅓ cup shredded natural Swiss cheese
3 tablespoons minced green onions, white part only	1 tablespoon butter

Preheat oven to moderate (375°).

Combine wine, salt, pepper, bay leaf, and onion in a wide saucepan; heat to simmering. Add scallops and mushrooms (if necessary, add enough water to cover ingredients); cover, and simmer for 5 minutes. With a slotted spoon, remove scallops and mushrooms. For Sauce Parisienne, cook remaining liquid over high heat, stirring occasionally, until reduced to 1 cup; remove bay leaf.

Cut scallops crosswise into ¼-inch-thick slices. Fold scallops into two-thirds of the Sauce Parisienne, and turn into 6 oiled baking dishes (preferably ones that are scallop shells). Spoon remaining sauce over the top; sprinkle with cheese and dot with butter. Place dishes on a tray or broiling pan. Bake until heated through, about 10 minutes. Then slip under broiler to lightly brown on top. 4 servings.

Sauce Parisienne

¼ cup butter
¼ cup flour
1 cup cooking liquid from scallops
¾ cup milk

2 egg yolks
½ cup heavy cream
Salt and freshly ground black pepper to taste
Few drops of fresh lemon juice

In a saucepan over medium heat, melt butter; add flour and stir to make a smooth paste. Remove from heat, and gradually stir in liquid from scallops and milk. Return to heat and cook, whisking, until thickened and smooth.

In a large mixing bowl, beat egg yolks with cream; gradually beat in the hot sauce. Return to saucepan and cook, whisking, until mixture boils; then simmer for 1 minute. Season to taste with salt, pepper, and lemon juice.

BASIC WINE CHOICE: Fruity white

Sweet in taste and dense in texture, scallops have an uncanny way of causing good wine to taste like cod liver oil. The only way to get around the problem is with a genuinely tart wine (the wine can be a bit sweet into the bargain, but not only sweet). In general, Johannisbergs are the best choice; Ste. Michelle's Johannisberg Riesling from Washington State does the job superbly.

93

10

Poultry

Wine cooks into chicken dishes in the usual ways—as a baste, as a marinade, or as part of a sauce. While the flavors of most meats dominate the taste of a finished dish, the light flavor of chicken almost disappears in favor of other ingredients. Because of this, it is those other ingredients that govern the choice of wine both in the preparation and the eating of chicken.

Having only a few light herbs in a chicken dish means you will use a light white wine in it. Creamy ingredients usually require a richer white. Tomato sauce, or anything like it, makes red wine the sensible choice to add to the dish. (Mother Nature must have had savory sauces in mind when she designed the chicken with its firm meat and bland flavor.)

The choices are similar when considering the correct wine to drink with a chicken dish. Chicken all alone should be accompanied by the most delicate of white wines. Once sauced, however, the flavor of the chicken is less important than the flavor of the sauce when choosing a wine. As the recipes in this chapter demonstrate, the elegant cream sauces call for white wines; the robust spicy sauces, for reds. Herb bastes may call for either.

We have limited the recipes in the chapter to chicken for the simple reason that most other poultry is of such specific flavor that it profits little or none from the addition of wine in cooking. However, the wine that you drink with the more flavorful birds benefits them beyond measure. More than one winemaster traditionally celebrates Thanksgiving with roast turkey and a bottle of Chardonnay. A duckling—dripping fat—becomes twice as agreeable in the company of a tart young Cabernet or Zinfandel. Game birds need silky old Pinot Noirs or Cabernet Sauvignons.

Brandied Apricot Chicken Sauté

Chicken Breasts in Tarragon Cream

Chicken Tetrazzini

Mushroom-smothered Sherry Chicken

Rosé-glazed Chicken

Coq au Vin

Rosemary Roasted Chicken

Brandied Apricot Chicken Sauté

By classic definition, chicken sauté simply means chicken browned in shortening and then covered and cooked slowly with seasonings. In this recipe, apricot becomes a most unusual seasoning. Wine and brandy serve as the bridge that brings bird and fruit together to a savory whole.

The flavor of brandy, incidentally, changes dramatically with flaming, growing darker and richer. Here, the brandy flavor floats up as an aromatic haze enveloping the whole dish.

If it can be arranged, use bananas somewhere else in the menu. They provide an intriguing counterpoint to the apricot in the sauté sauce.

¾ **cup dry white wine**
12 **moist dried apricot halves**
 2 **whole large chicken breasts,**
   split, boned, and skinned, if
   you wish (4 breast pieces)
Salt and freshly ground black
   pepper to taste
¼ **teaspoon crumbled dried thyme**

¼ **cup butter**
¼ **cup minced green onions,**
   with part of green tops
⅓ **cup brandy**
 1 **teaspoon fresh lemon juice**
 6 **tablespoons chopped, lightly**
   toasted filberts (hazelnuts)

Heat wine (do not boil); pour over apricots in a bowl and let stand for 1 hour. Drain wine and reserve.

Rinse chicken and dry well. Sprinkle generously with salt and pepper to season and with thyme. Fold loose corners of each piece under to form a compact piece of meat. In a large heavy skillet, melt butter; quickly brown chicken on both sides in it. Reduce heat to low. Stir onion into butter, and add apricots.

Warm brandy in a small pan, light it, and pour it over chicken. Gently tilt skillet back and forth until flames die. Add ¼ cup of the reserved wine. Cover, and cook over low heat until chicken loses translucency and is tender, about 10 minutes. Remove chicken to warmed serving plates or platter; keep warm.

Add remaining wine and lemon juice to apricots and pan drippings, and cook, gently stirring, over high heat until liquid cooks down to a sauce of thin syrup consistency. Pour over chicken, and sprinkle with filberts. 4 servings.

BASIC WINE CHOICE: Fruity white

The Chenin Blancs of Mirassou and Paul Masson are white wines that are frankly sweet but not at all cloying. Johannisberg Rieslings would be drier alternatives. Whatever wine you choose, it has to be stoutly flavored to hold its own against this dish.

Chicken Breasts in Tarragon Cream

Sheer simplicity of flavors reigns in this dish. The brandy in the sauce nudges both the wine and the delicate tang of tarragon to a little more prominence than they would attain without it.

2 whole large chicken breasts, split, boned, and skinned (4 breast pieces)
Salt and freshly ground black pepper to taste
3 tablespoons butter
1 tablespoon minced shallots
½ cup dry white wine
About 2 teaspoons crumbled dried tarragon
¾ cup heavy cream
1½ teaspoons brandy
2 teaspoons finely minced fresh parsley

Rinse chicken and dry well.

Sprinkle chicken generously with salt and lightly with pepper to season. Melt butter in a large heavy skillet over medium heat; add chicken, and brown on both sides, about 10 minutes total. Stir shallots into butter. Add 2 tablespoons of the wine. Cover and cook over low heat just until chicken loses translucency and is tender, about 5 minutes. Remove chicken to warm serving plates or platter; keep warm.

Add remaining wine, tarragon, cream, and brandy to pan. Then cook and stir over high heat until liquid reduces to consistency of heavy cream. Taste and correct seasoning, and stir in parsley. Pour over chicken. 2 or 4 servings.

BASIC WINE CHOICE: Fruity white

A fruity wine has to be somewhat sweet to taste balanced. The basic problem here is to avoid too sweet a wine (which destroys the subtle flavor of tarragon), and yet not get a bone-dry wine (which lacks springy lilt). The following wines all walk an appropriate tightrope: The Christian Brothers' Pineau de la Loire, Souverain Cellar's Pineau Souverain, and Charles Krug's, Beringer's, and Robert Mondavi's Fumé Blanc. At less expense, generics such as Italian Swiss Colony's Gold Chablis and Gallo's Chablis Blanc match up nicely.

97

Chicken Tetrazzini

The story goes that around the turn of the century, the chef of the Palace Hotel in San Francisco created Chicken Tetrazzini in honor of the Italian coloratura soprano Luisa Tetrazzini.

Today, some versions of the dish call for white wine as the wine ingredient, and some call for dry sherry. We like to use both—mostly white but enough sherry to boost the flavor.

If your starting point should be cooked chicken (or turkey) meat instead of a whole uncooked chicken, you will need about four cups of slivered meat.

1 stewing chicken, about 4 to 5 pounds	½ cup dry white wine
1 teaspoon salt	1 egg yolk, lightly beaten
1 large parsley sprig	¾ to 1 cup shredded or grated Parmesan cheese, divided
1 bay leaf	3 tablespoons dry sherry
1 stalk celery with leaves, sliced	1½ teaspoons finely grated onion
1 large onion, quartered	¼ teaspoon ground nutmeg
About 10 whole black peppercorns	Dash of Tabasco
3 whole cloves	Freshly ground black pepper
¾ pound fresh mushrooms, thinly sliced	6 ounces packaged dried spaghetti (or tagliarini)
½ cup butter, divided	About ⅓ cup sliced almonds
6 tablespoons flour	
1 cup dairy half-and-half (light cream)	

Rinse chicken.

Cut chicken into pieces and put into a large kettle. Add water to cover, salt, parsley, bay leaf, celery, onion quarters, peppercorns, and cloves. Cover and simmer until meat is very tender, about 1½ hours. Allow chicken to cool slightly in broth before removing. Remove skin from meat and meat from bones, discarding skin and bones; break meat into large slivers. Strain broth, and skim off fat.

Preheat oven to moderate (375°). In a skillet, sauté mushrooms in 3 tablespoons of the butter until tender; set aside.

Melt 4 tablespoons of the butter in a large saucepan. Add flour, and stir to make a smooth paste. Gradually add 3 cups of the chicken broth, the half-and-half, and then the white wine, whisking and cooking to make a smooth, thickened sauce. Remove from heat. Beat a little of the hot sauce into the egg yolk. Gradually whisk egg yolk mixture back into sauce. Stir in ½ cup of the Parmesan and the sherry, grated onion, nutmeg, Tabasco, and pepper. Correct seasoning. Measure out 1 cup of the sauce and set aside.

Cook spaghetti in boiling salted water just until tender; rinse and drain.

Fold chicken, mushrooms, and spaghetti into remaining large portion of sauce. Turn into a 2½-quart, oiled shallow baking dish. Pour reserved sauce evenly over top. Sprinkle with remaining Parmesan and the almonds, and dot with remaining 1 tablespoon butter. Bake until heated through and bubbling, about 20 to 30 minutes. Slip under broiler to lightly brown. 6 to 8 servings.

BASIC WINE CHOICE: Fruity white

Johannisberg Riesling suits Chicken Tetrazzini both as a flavor and as a moderately lavish companion to a moderately lavish dish. We admire the one from Heitz Cellars with this dish.

Mushroom-smothered Sherry Chicken

Few dishes allow the wine ingredient to dominate as much as it does in this rich casserole. Yet the nutty flavor of good sherry does not wear out its welcome as the single most prominent taste.

Since this can be assembled several hours ahead of serving time and then baked in time for dinner, it is easy to do for company.

3 pounds frying chicken pieces, preferably breasts and thighs
Salt and freshly ground black pepper to taste
Paprika
About ¼ cup butter, divided
¾ cup very finely chopped onions

¾ pound fresh mushrooms, sliced
3 tablespoons flour
1 cup chicken broth
½ cup dry sherry
1¼ teaspoons crumbled dried rosemary

Preheat oven to moderate (375°).

Rinse chicken and dry well. Sprinkle generously with salt, pepper, and paprika to season. In large heavy skillet over medium heat, melt 2 to 3 tablespoons butter; add chicken pieces and brown. Remove to a 3-quart shallow casserole with tight-fitting cover.

Add onion and mushrooms to skillet and sauté until onions are limp. Sprinkle with flour and stir; then add chicken broth, sherry, and rosemary. Cook, stirring, for a few minutes until liquid is blended and slightly thickened; pour over chicken. Cover and bake for 40 minutes, or until chicken is tender. 6 servings.

BASIC WINE CHOICE: Full dry white

Sauvignon Blanc is not often made dry, but when it is—as is Wente's—it carries enough authority to compete with the sherry in the dish. Pinot Blanc mates well, too. Dry Semillon (or, as it is often labeled, dry sauterne) serves well for those who do not admire austerity in white wine.

Rosé-glazed Chicken

Fruit is the force in this dish. Although the rosy glaze is quite sweet, fruit and oven heat join with the chicken to keep the overall effect of the dish savory.

A good accompaniment is split and buttered corn muffins with watercress tucked inside.

3 pounds frying chicken pieces, preferably breasts and thighs
Salt to taste

About 2 tablespoons salad oil
About 2 tablespoons butter
Rosé Plum Glaze (recipe follows)

Preheat oven to moderate (375°).

Rinse chicken and dry well. Sprinkle generously with salt. Heat oil and butter together in a large heavy skillet; add chicken and brown quickly on all sides. Arrange chicken pieces in a single layer in an oiled shallow baking pan. Spoon Rosé Plum Glaze over chicken. Bake for 35 minutes, or until chicken is tender. 4 to 6 servings.

NOTE: You can charcoal-broil this chicken instead of oven-glazing it. Rinse chicken and dry well; sprinkle generously with salt. Place chicken on oiled grill, skin side up, about 6 inches above coals giving off medium heat. Cook, turning with tongs and basting frequently with Rosé Plum Glaze, for about 45 minutes, or until chicken is tender and glaze is set.

Rosé Plum Glaze

1 jar (10 ounces) plum jam
¼ cup rosé wine
1 teaspoon grated onion
1 teaspoon grated fresh lemon peel
½ teaspoon crushed whole anise seeds
½ teaspoon ground ginger

½ teaspoon dry mustard
¼ teaspoon salt
¼ teaspoon freshly ground black pepper
¼ teaspoon ground cinnamon
⅛ teaspoon ground cloves
Generous dash of Tabasco

Stir all ingredients together thoroughly.

BASIC WINE CHOICE: Rosé

The kind of rosé you choose depends entirely on whether you prefer sweeter or drier rosés. The former are usually labeled vin rosé and Grenache Rosé. Drier ones come from grapes generally used to make red wines—Zinfandel Rosé, Grignolino Rosé, and Petite Rosé (from Petite Sirah grapes); these are harder to find.

The advent of faintly bubbly pink Chablis provides another choice. Bubbles freshen flavors a bit, especially when the wine is chilled deeply.

Coq au Vin

There are numerous, varying recipes for Coq au Vin. But for any rendition, the necessary ingredients for the dish—besides chicken—are onions, mushrooms, and bacon. And the essential method is that the chicken be simmered in wine—sometimes white, but far more usually red.

When wine is thus the simmering liquid, it cooks for a long enough time so that its flavor changes. In fact, wine does not appear as an identifiable flavor in the finished dish, though certainly it enriches the whole effect.

French-cut green beans are a good vegetable to serve with this.

3 ounces lean bacon, cut into
  thin strips
6 tablespoons butter, divided
1 frying chicken, about 3 pounds
About ½ teaspoon salt
⅛ teaspoon freshly ground
  black pepper
¼ cup brandy
2½ cups dry red wine
¾ cup regular-strength beef
  broth or stock
1 large clove garlic, minced
  or mashed

½ teaspoon crumbled dried
  thyme
1 bay leaf
About 1½ tablespoons finely
  chopped fresh parsley,
  divided
2½ tablespoons flour
½ pound fresh mushrooms,
  thinly sliced
2 tablespoons minced shallots
Browned Onions (recipe follows)

Cook bacon in boiling water for 5 minutes; drain, and dry on paper towels. In a large heavy skillet over medium heat, melt 2 tablespoons of the butter; add bacon and sauté until lightly browned. Remove with a slotted spoon and set aside.

Wipe chicken dry, cut into serving pieces, and quickly brown on all sides in same skillet; sprinkle chicken with salt and pepper. Return bacon to pan. Cover, and cook over low heat for about 10 minutes; turn chicken once.

Warm brandy in a small pan, ignite it, and pour over chicken. Gently tilt skillet back and forth until flames die. Remove chicken and bacon, and arrange in a baking–serving casserole dish with cover.

Preheat oven to moderate (350°).

Add to skillet the wine, broth, garlic, thyme, bay leaf, and 1 tablespoon of the parsley. Cook over high heat, stirring, until reduced to 2¼ cups. Mix flour with 2 tablespoons softened butter to make a paste. Remove wine mixture from heat, and quickly whisk in flour mixture. Return to heat, and boil gently until thickened and smooth, about 2 minutes. Taste and correct seasoning. Pour sauce over chicken. Cover chicken tightly, and bake for 30 minutes.

Meanwhile, in another skillet, sauté mushrooms and shallots in the remaining 2 tablespoons of butter until lightly browned. When chicken has baked for 30 minutes, gently stir in mushrooms, shallots, and Browned Onions, spooning sauce over them. Return to oven and bake, uncovered, for about 5 to 10 minutes more, or until chicken is tender. Remove bay leaf; sprinkle chicken with remaining parsley. 4 servings.

Browned Onions

1 tablespoon olive oil
1 tablespoon butter

12 to 16 tiny white onions (about 1 inch in diameter), peeled

Preheat oven to moderate (350°).

Heat oil and butter in a heavy skillet over medium heat. Add onions and brown on all sides, rolling onions to brown as evenly as possible, about 10 minutes total. Put onions in small baking dish (or keep in skillet, if possible). Bake, uncovered, until onions are very tender but still retain shape, about 30 minutes; turn occasionally.

BASIC WINE CHOICE: Fruity red

103

Coq au Vin got off to a humble start in the Auvergne in France, so it owes some of its character to the everyday wines of that region. It has picked up polish along the way. In the form it shows here, it fits with Gamay, Gamay Beaujolais, Gamay Noir, and Pinot St. George. Sebastiani's Gamay Beaujolais is exemplary. Cool the bottle in the refrigerator for half an hour before serving, or bring it out of a cool cellar just in time to sit down at the table. Cooling is a good old country trick for bringing the fruit flavors of red wine into fuller focus.

Rosemary Roasted Chicken

The usual herb for chicken is tarragon. But we use rosemary here with great success—perhaps because it is such a surprise.

The white wine and butter baste ensures a brilliant glaze finish (red wine can discolor the chicken skin).

1 roasting chicken, about
  4 pounds
About 3 tablespoons dry white
  wine, divided
Salt and freshly ground black
  pepper to taste
About 6 tablespoons soft
  butter, divided

Fresh rosemary sprigs or ½
  teaspoon crumbled dried
  rosemary, divided
¼ teaspoon salt
¼ teaspoon freshly ground
  black pepper

Preheat oven to moderate (375°).

Remove excess body fat from chicken cavity; wash chicken and pat dry. Rub cavity well with 1 tablespoon of the wine, and sprinkle lightly with salt and pepper. Put 2 tablespoons of the butter and a rosemary sprig (or ¼ teaspoon dried rosemary) into cavity. Truss and tie chicken. Rub entire surface with about 2 tablespoons of the butter. Place on rack in a roasting pan; roast for 1 hour.

Melt remaining butter, and stir in the remaining wine, ¼ teaspoon each of salt and pepper, and ½ teaspoon snipped fresh rosemary (or ¼ teaspoon dried); brush over chicken. Continue roasting chicken, basting with wine mixture, for 30 to 40 minutes more, or until leg and thigh joint move easily and juices that run out of punctured thigh are clear. Cut chicken into quarters with poultry shears, or carve. Serve with pan juices spooned over. 4 servings.

BASIC WINE CHOICE: Fruity red

The wine ingredient in this recipe is exposed to a lot of high, dry heat, which causes substantial alteration in the wine's flavor. The changed flavor makes it possible to select a red wine to drink.

A Gamay or Burgundy will stand up to the pungency of rosemary; so will a young Zinfandel. We recommend, in particular, The Christian Brother's Gamay Noir.

104

Brandied Apricot Chicken Sauté, p. 96

11

Beef

First-rate beef does not really need wine in the cooking (although wine with dinner is its most handsome complement). Rather, the inexpensive cuts of beef are the ones that call for wine during the cooking—the practical effect being to tenderize, the artistic one to flavor. This assemblage of recipes pays particular homage to the role of wine in elevating the humbler cuts from the cow into noteworthy foods. The chapter focuses on tenderizing marinades and those savory sauces that keep beef interesting when it has to be chewed a little longer than usual.

As for wines to drink, almost any red will mate harmoniously with almost any beef. So will some white wines. No other meat is so generously suited to wine. This is to say not that there is no correct wine to drink with beef but that it is mainly a matter of personal prejudice. Some people like astringent wines, wines that pucker the palate; they lean toward Cabernet Sauvignon for festive beef dinners, or Zinfandel for more casual meals. Others do not like astringency much at all, preferring Pinot Noir or one of the Gamays or an occasional white wine with their beef.

Inexpensive beef dishes suggest lower-priced wines to drink.

Hamburgers Burgundy

Rahela, a wonderful cook in Dubrovnik, Yugoslavia, says that just the littlest sugar in a ground beef mixture makes it better; the sugar "takes away the meat sour." Alice Heitz, wife of Napa Valley wine maker Joe Heitz, says that marinating hamburger in a smooth red wine before barbecuing improves the flavor. This recipe combines both thoughts.

1½ **pounds ground beef chuck**	¼ **cup minced green onions, with**
¾ **teaspoon salt**	**part of green tops**
½ **teaspoon freshly ground black**	2 **ounces blue cheese, cut into**
pepper	**4 thin slices**
¼ **teaspoon sugar**	⅔ **cup dry red wine**
¼ **cup chopped fresh parsley**	4 **slices bacon (optional)**

In a large bowl, mix chuck, salt, pepper, sugar, parsley, and onion. Lightly shape into eight ½-inch-thick patties.

To make *each* serving, place 2 patties together, enclosing between them a thin slice of cheese; pinch at edges to seal cheese in well. Repeat to make 3 more large patties.

Place hamburgers in a shallow pan, and pour wine over. Chill for 2 hours, turning once. If you wish, encircle each hamburger with a bacon slice and secure with toothpicks. Remove from wine, and broil over hot coals to doneness you wish. 4 servings.

BASIC WINE CHOICE: Mellow red

Wines that remain a bit sweet have their place; one of the places is with hamburger, and especially this hamburger. Try serving Gallo's Hearty Burgundy, Guild Vino da Tavola, or Italian Swiss Colony's Burgundy. If the day is warm, chill the wine slightly.

108

Herbed Wine Meat Loaf

The red wine added to this meat loaf moistens and lightly flavors the meat. The wine in the chili-sauce condiment mellows the sharpness of the sauce alone and points up a slight wine flavor overall.

A good side dish of vegetables is buttered green beans or corn.

½ cup fine dry bread crumbs
1 cup dry red wine, divided
3 tablespoons butter
1 large onion, finely chopped
1 pound ground beef chuck
½ pound ground veal
½ pound ground lean pork
2 eggs, lightly beaten
⅓ cup finely chopped fresh parsley
1½ teaspoons salt
½ teaspoon freshly ground black pepper

½ teaspoon crumbled dried basil
¼ teaspoon crumbled dried thyme
⅛ teaspoon crumbled dried marjoram
⅛ teaspoon ground allspice
1 bay leaf, finely crumbled
1 large clove garlic, minced or mashed
3 to 4 slices lean bacon
Chili-Wine Sauce (recipe follows)

Preheat oven to moderate (350°).

In a bowl, soak bread crumbs in ¾ cup of the wine until soft. In a skillet, melt butter; add onion and sauté until tender.

In a large bowl, lightly but thoroughly mix all ingredients *except* the remaining ¼ cup of wine, bacon, and the Chili-Wine Sauce. Gently press mixture into a 5- x 9-inch loaf pan. Pour on as much remaining wine as loaf will absorb. Cover with bacon.

Bake for 1½ hours. During baking, baste with remaining wine, which has been warmed. Let loaf stand for a few minutes, and then thickly slice. Pass the Chili-Wine Sauce. 5 to 6 servings.

Chili-Wine Sauce

½ cup chili sauce   ¼ cup dry red wine

Stir ingredients together, and serve at room temperature or slightly warmed.

BASIC WINE CHOICE: Fruity red

The United States produces literally dozens of good, sound red wines under the name of Burgundy. Happily, quite a few of them come in gallon jugs. People dedicated to dry wine should seek, for this kind of meal, a Burgundy from one of California's coast counties wineries. People who like just a hint of sweet in their Burgundy should obtain one from a large California producer or from a producer in the northeastern states where native American grapes and their hybrids regularly yield somewhat sweet reds.

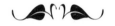

Harolyn's Semi-Classical Beef Burgundy
(Boeuf Bourguignonne)

Classical Beef Burgundy would not contain sherry, Worcestershire sauce, and catsup. Otherwise, this recipe is much the same as the one that is indigenous to the French Burgundy countryside.

When you make this stew, you use two wine cookery techniques —simmering and finishing—in the same dish. And you have the perfect chance to see how greatly wine flavor changes during long, slow heating. Taste the wine before you put it into the pot, and then taste the wine ingredient in the juices at the end of the cooking time. The change, as you will see, is enough so that you will want an added wine finish for the juices. The finish (the two tablespoons of wine added at the last) again emphasizes that wine gives the dish its definition and character.

As is true of many stews, this one is even better when you make it a day ahead, chill it, and then reheat it before serving.

Serve in deeply rimmed dinner plates or shallow soup plates. Accompany with crusty French bread.

3 tablespoons butter
2 pounds lean boneless beef chuck, cut into 1½-inch cubes
⅓ cup dry sherry
1 large onion, finely chopped
¾ pound fresh mushrooms, sliced ⅛ inch thick
1 large clove garlic, minced or mashed
1 tablespoon catsup
1 tablespoon Worcestershire sauce
¼ cup flour
1 cup regular-strength beef broth or stock

3 cups dry red wine, divided
About ½ teaspoon salt
½ teaspoon crumbled dried thyme
½ teaspoon crumbled dried basil
½ teaspoon crumbled dried chervil
About ¼ teaspoon freshly ground black pepper
1 large bay leaf
About 1 tablespoon chopped fresh parsley (preferably flat-leaved Italian parsley)

In a large heavy deep skillet with cover, melt butter; add meat and brown over medium-high heat. Reduce heat to medium. Add sherry. Push meat to one side of pan. Add onion, and cook until limp, about 5 minutes. Add mushrooms, and cook until barely tender, about 3 minutes. Add garlic.

Stir together catsup, Worcestershire, flour, and beef broth. Add to pan, and stir and cook until ingredients are blended and juices begin to boil and thicken. Stir in all except 2 tablespoons of the wine, the salt, thyme, basil, chervil, pepper, and bay leaf.

Cover tightly, and simmer over very low heat for 3 hours, or until meat is very tender; stir occasionally. Correct seasoning with salt and pepper. Just before serving, stir in remaining 2 tablespoons wine. Sprinkle with parsley. 4 servings.

BASIC WINE CHOICE: Fruity red

The original idea of the dish was economy. In Burgundy, farm villagers use a common wine not only in the making of this dish, but also in the drinking. Since our version is slightly more elegant, we usually choose a Zinfandel for guests who favor astringent wines and a Gamay for those who prefer softer reds.

Braised Beef in Red Wine

Wine makes a full impression on a good pot-roast cut of beef, in that it seasons, tenderizes, and forms much of the saucing.

Boiled new potatoes go well with this dish; for dessert, a good cheese is right.

1 rump pot roast of beef, about 4 pounds, well trimmed
Salad oil or lard
1 large onion, thinly sliced
2 stalks celery, thinly sliced
2 large carrots, peeled and thinly sliced
¼ cup chopped fresh parsley
1¼ teaspoons crumbled dried thyme
About 1 teaspoon salt
About ¼ teaspoon freshly ground black pepper

¼ teaspoon ground nutmeg
Pinch of ground cloves
1 bay leaf
1 large clove garlic, minced or mashed
1½ teaspoons grated fresh orange peel
2 cups dry red wine
1 cup canned condensed beef consommé, undiluted
⅓ cup brandy
Finely chopped pistachio nuts or parsley sprigs

Wipe beef dry. In a large heavy kettle or Dutch oven over medium heat, brown beef well on all sides in a small amount of oil. Drain any fat in excess of 1 tablespoon. Add onion, celery, carrots, and chopped parsley, and lightly brown. Add all remaining ingredients except pistachio nuts.

Cover kettle tightly, and slowly simmer until meat is very tender, about 3 to 4 hours; turn meat occasionally. Remove meat. Skim any excess fat off top of juices; taste juices and correct seasoning. Thinly slice meat across the grain. Ladle juices and vegetables over meat as a sauce. Sprinkle with pistachios or garnish with parsley sprigs. 8 servings.

BASIC WINE CHOICE: Full, dry red

Most of the classic recipes of *haute cuisine* graduated from country origins. This beef dish has traveled most of the distance from a country kitchen to a Cordon Bleu one. The wine that goes with it logically would be a Pinot Noir, but not the rarest treasure in your cellar. A good, medium-priced, nonvintage bottling will grace the meal nicely and be appropriate with the cheese course afterward; we are fond of the Pinot Noirs from The Christian Brothers, Paul Masson, and Sonoma Vineyards (Windsor).

Beef and Onion Red Wine Stew

Though we do not know precisely where the dish, or the idea, of a French *estouffade,* a Greek *stefado,* an Italian *stufato,* and a Spanish *estofado* began, we do know that the definitions everywhere almost always depend upon the stewing together of beef, onions, and red wine.

A good salad with the stew is one made of butter or Boston lettuce, fresh nectarines or peaches, a few orange slices, and an oil–vinegar–lemon–juice dressing seasoned with basil.

4 **thin slices lean bacon, cut crosswise into ¼-inch strips**
3 **pounds lean beef stew meat, cut into 1½-inch cubes**
About 3 tablespoons olive oil
½ **teaspoon salt**
¼ **teaspoon freshly ground black pepper**
1 **medium onion, chopped**
½ **can (6-ounce size) tomato paste**

About 2¼ cups dry red wine, divided
2 **cloves garlic, minced or mashed**
2 **bay leaves**
About ¾ cup regular-strength beef broth or stock
1½ **pounds tiny white onions (about 1 inch in diameter), peeled**

113

Cook bacon in boiling water for 3 minutes; drain and reserve.

In a large heavy kettle or Dutch oven, over medium to medium-high heat, brown beef on all sides in oil; sprinkle with salt and pepper. Add the chopped onion, and sauté until limp. Mix together tomato paste and 1 cup of the wine; pour over meat. Add garlic, bay leaves, and bacon.

Cover kettle tightly, and simmer for 1½ hours; add remaining wine and the broth, a little at a time, during this cooking. Add tiny onions, cover, and simmer for 1½ hours more, or until onions and meat are very tender. Add salt to taste. 6 servings.

BASIC WINE CHOICE: Full, dry red

Perhaps it is only because of the power of suggestion aroused by the Mediterranean origins of *estouffade,* but wines from Mediterranean grape varieties seem to fare best with this dish. In particular, the smooth riches of a Petite Sirah are welcome accompaniment to the similar richness in the stew, while a Barbera is a very close second choice.

Cheese-crusted Swiss Steak

In this version of an old favorite, onions run deeper as a flavor than in most Swiss steaks because you cook the onions separately into a sauce before combining and cooking with the meat. The breadth of this beef seasoning capitalizes on the natural affinities of cheese and red wine, and beef and onions.

Hot fresh spinach is a good side dish.

2½ **pounds top round steak,**	2 **tablespoons butter**
cut 2 inches thick	**Onion-Wine Sauce (recipe**
2 **tablespoons flour**	**follows)**
1 **teaspoon salt**	3 **to 4 tablespoons grated or**
About ¼ **teaspoon freshly**	**shredded Parmesan cheese**
ground black pepper	**Finely chopped fresh parsley**

Making diagonal cuts about ½ inch deep and 1 inch apart, score steak on both sides. Mix flour, salt, and pepper, and rub well into both sides of meat.

In a large heavy skillet with cover, melt butter; add steak and brown well on both sides over medium heat. Drain any excess fat. Add Onion-Wine Sauce, cover tightly, and simmer until meat is very tender, about 1½ to 2 hours; stir sauce occasionally.

Remove steak to a warm broiling–serving platter. Spoon enough sauce over top of steak to coat. Sprinkle with Parmesan, and slip under preheated broiler until lightly browned. Sprinkle lightly with parsley. Taste remaining onion sauce and generously add salt to season. Slice steak, and serve with sauce. 6 servings.

Onion-Wine Sauce

3 **tablespoons butter**	½ **teaspoon crumbled dried**
4 **large onions, finely chopped**	**marjoram**
3 **tablespoons flour**	¼ **teaspoon crumbled dried**
1 **teaspoon sugar**	**thyme**
1 **can (10½ ounces) beef**	¼ **teaspoon ground ginger**
bouillon, undiluted	⅛ **teaspoon ground nutmeg**
1 **cup dry red wine**	1 **large clove garlic, minced**
1 **tablespoon tomato paste**	**or mashed**

In a heavy kettle, melt butter; add onion and sauté over medium-high heat until browned. Stir in flour and sugar; sauté, stirring, until flour browns in bottom of kettle. Add bouillon and wine; stir to loosen browned flour. Add remaining ingredients and cook, stirring, until blended, about 5 minutes.

Even though onions dominate the flavor of this Swiss steak, they do so gently. The lightest of Gamays or Gamay Beaujolais are excellent companions, especially those of Beaulieu, Charles Krug, Mirassou, and Sebastiani.

Sautéed Steak

This recipe is for the simple cooking of steaks of good quality. It is followed by recipes for two traditional red wine sauces to be used with the sautéed steaks. The same wine choice suits either recipe rendition.

4 small boneless broiling steaks (such as filet mignon, boneless club, Delmonico), each about ½ pound, cut 1 inch thick, and well trimmed	**About 1½ tablespoons olive oil** **About 1½ tablespoons butter** **Salt and freshly ground black pepper to taste**

Make small cuts through any gristle edges of each steak to prevent curling. Wipe steaks dry.

Heat oil and butter in a large heavy skillet over medium-high heat until butter foams. When butter begins to stop foaming, add steaks. Sauté until browned on both sides and done to your liking, turning only once; sauté about 3 minutes on each side for rare steak (if necessary, make a small cut in steak to check dóneness).

Remove steaks to warmed serving plates or platter. Season with salt and pepper; keep warm. Finish with one of the next two recipes for sauces. 4 servings.

Wine and Butter Sauce

This steak sauce demonstrates the process of deglazing the pan with wine. You add the wine to the crusty drippings remaining in the pan from sautéing the meat; then as you cook and stir over high heat, the wine loosens the drippings, blends with them, and cooks down or reduces enough to become a thin sauce for the steaks. When the wine is subjected to such a high heat, its flavor changes greatly.

¾ cup dry red wine   **3 to 4 tablespoons soft butter**

Remove excess fat from skillet used for cooking steaks. Add wine, and stir over high heat to loosen drippings; cook until reduced to about 3 tablespoons and of a thin syrup consistency. Remove from heat and stir in butter, about 1 tablespoon at a time (butter should be of a thick creamy consistency; do not let it melt down to a thin liquid). Pour sauce over sautéed steaks. 4 servings.

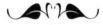

Sauce Marchand de Vins

This is simply an extension of the Wine and Butter Sauce, made slightly more complex by the addition of shallots, parsley, and more butter.

1½ tablespoons butter	**Salt and freshly ground black**
3 tablespoons minced shallots	**pepper to taste**
½ cup dry red wine	**2 tablespoons minced fresh**
6 tablespoons soft butter	**parsley**

Remove excess fat from skillet used for cooking steaks. Add the 1½ tablespoons butter and melt it. Add shallots, and sauté just to cloak with butter and to cook through. Add wine, and stir over high heat to loosen drippings; cook until reduced to a thin syrup consistency.

Remove pan from heat, and stir in soft butter, about 1 tablespoon at a time (butter should be of a thick creamy consistency; do not let it melt down to a thin liquid). Season sauce with salt and pepper; stir in parsley. Spoon over sautéed steaks. 4 servings.

BASIC WINE CHOICE: Full, dry red

This is a hang-the-expense sort of meal. More important, the rich, buttery flavors reach such a point of elegance that the finest of wines are the only correct ones. Our choices are Cabernet Sauvignon or Pinot Noir, preferably vintage-dated ones with several years behind them; in either case, search out Beaulieu, Heitz Cellars, Inglenook, Louis M. Martini, Robert Mondavi, Souverain, or a peer.

Wine-Marinade-basted Barbecue Steaks

As part of this marinade, wine seasons and tenderizes the beef. The same marinade then becomes a barbecue baste, and the wine continues to season.

On a summer evening, you might serve as a surrounding menu hot green beans with basil, sesame-buttered French bread, and fresh melon wedges.

⅓ cup dry rosé or dry red wine	½ teaspoon crumbled dried thyme
¼ cup olive oil	¼ teaspoon freshly ground black pepper
½ teaspoon fresh lemon juice	1 bay leaf, finely crumbled
1 large clove garlic, minced or mashed	2 tablespoons minced fresh parsley
½ teaspoon salt	4 thick steaks for barbecuing
½ teaspoon dry mustard	

Combine all ingredients, except steaks, and beat together with a fork. Pour over steaks and marinate at room temperature; marinate 1-inch-thick steaks for 1 hour and thicker steaks longer.

Pour off marinade and reserve. Barbecue steaks on greased grill over glowing charcoal to doneness you desire; turn only once. Baste with marinade. Steaks may be cooked to desired doneness but are best when fairly rare. 4 servings.

117

BASIC WINE CHOICE: Fruity red

On most of the days of the year, a barbecued steak calls for whatever red is close at hand. But on the sweltering nights of summer when barbecuing is an escape from the kitchen more than a planned pleasure, the wine that helps beat the heat is a dry rosé that you can chill to the bone before drinking. The driest California rosés are varietals, especially Zinfandel Rosé and Grignolino Rosé.

Steak Sauce Provençale

Choose small broiling steaks of your favorite cut, or shape thick patties of chopped steak. Pan-broil steaks to the doneness you like, and keep them warm while you finish the sauce. If you enjoy an abundance of butter, increase it by two tablespoons.

A suggested vegetable is hot summer squash.

4 medium tomatoes, peeled, cut into sixths, and seeded
½ teaspoon sugar
½ cup butter, divided
¼ cup minced green onions, white part only
½ cup dry white wine
3 large cloves garlic, minced or mashed
5 tablespoons finely chopped fresh parsley, divided
Salt and freshly ground black pepper to taste

Sprinkle tomatoes with sugar and set aside.

In a large heavy skillet over medium heat, melt 2 tablespoons of the butter; add onion and just heat through. Add wine and cook, stirring, until slightly reduced. Add tomatoes and gently cook, turning, just until heated through; do not allow them to lose shape. Add the remaining butter, garlic, and 4 tablespoons of the parsley. Gently shake and tilt pan over heat to mix ingredients and just melt butter (butter should be of a thick creamy consistency; do not let it melt down to a thin liquid).

Remove pan from heat, and season sauce with salt and pepper. Pour over broiled steaks, sprinkle with remaining parsley. 4 servings.

118

BASIC WINE CHOICE: Full, dry white

Now and then combining a small, tender piece of beef and a delicate sauce encourages breaking the rule that red wine should be served with red meat. This is one of those times.

Chardonnays are the leading candidates because they are the most reliably dry and full of all the whites; we think first of those from Beaulieu and Mayacamas.

If scruple will not let you use white wine with red meat, turn to one of the Gamays.

Red Wine Meat Sauce for Pasta or Polenta

This mushroom- and meat-rich pasta sauce is meant mostly to sauce a narrowly stripped egg noodle, such as tagliarini, but you can use it over any pasta, such as spaghetti or fettuccine. Or you can layer it between ripples of cooked lasagne, top it with Parmesan cheese and butter dots, and bake it through. Or spoon it over polenta.

½ pound bulk pork sausage
1 pound ground round
2 very large onions, chopped
2 or 3 large cloves garlic, minced or mashed
½ cup chopped fresh parsley
½ pound fresh mushrooms, thinly sliced
3 cans (8 ounces each) tomato sauce
2 cups dry red wine
About 1 teaspoon salt

About ½ teaspoon ground sage
About ¼ teaspoon crumbled dried rosemary
¼ teaspoon crumbled dried marjoram
¼ teaspoon crumbled dried thyme
¼ teaspoon crumbled dried oregano
¼ teaspoon freshly ground black pepper

In a large heavy kettle or Dutch oven, slowly brown sausage; add ground round and brown. Add onion and sauté until limp. Add garlic, parsley, and mushrooms, and stir to coat with meat drippings. Stir in remaining ingredients.

Cover loosely and simmer, stirring occasionally, for about 3 hours, until sauce is reduced to a thick consistency. Makes about 2 quarts sauce, enough to top about 6 servings of pasta or polenta.

NOTE: You can make this sauce a few hours or a few days ahead and reheat before serving. To freeze sauce: Cool quickly and thoroughly, then ladle into freezer jars, cover tightly, and freeze. Before using, thaw and slowly reheat.

BASIC WINE CHOICE: Full, dry red

If friends or neighbors drop in for an informal company dinner, a Louis M. Martini or Sebastiani Barbera comes out of the cellar to drink with this dish. Barbera is usually described as "vinous," which is to say that it tastes winy rather than fruity or grapy. There is no easy explanation, but winy is a welcome quality when a rich meal of pasta wants a wine that will cut through both starch and tomato flavors. A less expensive alternative is Chianti.

Boiled Beef in White Wine Broth

Of all the ways to exalt the best of beef flavor, boiling (actually, simmering with a few judiciously chosen companions) may be the surest, for it brings the beef taste to prompt focus and does not fog it in any way.

You could use red wine in the broth, but white is better because it emphasizes the onion appropriately.

Offer coarse salt and horseradish on the side to be added with discretion.

1 boneless rump roast, about 4 pounds, very well trimmed
1½ teaspoons salt
1 cup dry white wine
1 teaspoon crumbled dried basil
½ teaspoon sugar
½ teaspoon crumbled dried thyme
¼ teaspoon freshly ground black pepper
1 large bay leaf
⅓ cup finely chopped fresh parsley

3 large carrots, peeled and diced
2 large turnips, peeled and diced
2 cups thinly sliced celery
2 medium onions, chopped
1 tablespoon tomato paste
½ pound fresh green beans, cut into 2-inch lengths and ends trimmed

Place beef in a large soup kettle. Add 7 cups cold water and salt. Heat to boiling; skim off film and discard. Add wine, basil, sugar, thyme, pepper, bay leaf, and parsley. Cover and simmer until meat is tender, about 3 hours or more; turn meat once or twice.

Add carrots, turnips, celery, and onion; cover again and simmer until vegetables are tender, about 30 minutes. Add tomato paste and green beans; cover and simmer until beans are tender, about 15 minutes more. Taste broth and correct seasoning. Remove beef, slice thinly, and arrange in large soup bowls. Ladle hot broth and vegetables over meat. 6 to 8 servings.

BASIC WINE CHOICE: Fruity red

A dry Burgundy goes handsomely with boiled beef. Ruby Cabernet is another choice, the most available bottling being Royal Host's (also labeled Pastene). The Ruby Cabernet grape was developed at the University of California specifically to grow in California's Central Valley.

120

A Many-Fish White-Wine Soup, p. 80

12

Veal

The flavor of veal is so delicate that it almost eludes description.

A cynical San Francisco gastronome contends that veal is beef for people who would rather eat chicken. This is true in the sense that veal shares chicken's capacity to complement a galaxy of sauces. But it is not true in the sense that the texture of veal is so specific that it cannot be mistaken for any other meat and that its total effect borders on the elegant.

The wise cook takes advantage of both the elusive and the elegant aspects of veal by combining it with a sauce but aiming for subtle refinements. Most of the classic sauces for veal require white wines; a few borrow the tawny riches of good, old dessert wines; only a handful of recipes call for reds.

As an ingredient, wine's great value is flavor. But because veal is often cooked for longer times than other meats in spite of its tendency to dry out, wine is also important as a moisturizer—both in sauces and as a baste.

The almost invariable choice of wine to drink with veal is a subtle, rather rich white. The wines made from grapes that originated in the Burgundy region of France seem to have particular affinity for veal, although on a number of occasions we have enjoyed a Johannisberg Riesling or a wine from one of the other Germanic grapes.

Veal Scaloppine
⤙ 124 ⤚

Braised Tarragon Veal Chops
⤙ 125 ⤚

Avocado Veal Sauté
⤙ 126 ⤚

Veal Roast with White Wine
⤙ 127 ⤚

Paprika Veal Casserole
⤙ 128 ⤚

Oven Stew of Veal in Red Wine
⤙ 129 ⤚

Brandied White Veal Stew
⤙ 130 ⤚

Veal Scaloppine

Tawny-hued dessert wines give a distinctly nutty flavor to various recipes for Veal Scaloppine. The Italians use Marsala because it is abundant there. Here, a medium-dry sherry serves the purpose just as well.

You can prepare the veal ahead through the point of adding consommé. Cover and chill; then reheat and finish the dish close to serving time. The egg yolk and cream finish is not required, but it does polish the dish with a satiny gloss.

We suggest fresh asparagus or spinach to go alongside.

2 pounds boneless veal cutlet, pounded very thin
Salt and freshly ground black pepper to taste
Flour
About 3 tablespoons olive oil
About 7 tablespoons butter, divided
½ pound fresh mushrooms, thinly sliced
⅓ cup minced green onions, with part of green tops

1¼ cups medium-dry sherry
½ teaspoon crumbled dried oregano
1 clove garlic, minced or mashed
½ can (10½-ounce size) condensed beef consommé, undiluted
1 egg yolk
1½ tablespoons heavy cream

Season veal with salt and pepper; coat with flour and shake off excess.

In a large, heavy skillet over medium heat, brown veal on both sides in olive oil and 3 tablespoons of the butter (brown only part of the veal at a time; do not crowd in pan). Remove veal from pan and set aside. In same skillet, sauté mushrooms in 2 tablespoons of the butter until tender; remove from pan and set aside. Melt 2 tablespoons more butter in same skillet; add onion, and sauté until limp. Stir in sherry, oregano, and garlic.

Return veal to the pan. Cook over medium heat, uncovered, until veal is tender and liquid almost disappears; turn veal gently to cook evenly on all sides. Return mushrooms to the pan, and add consommé. Simmer until liquid reduces to a sauce to just cloak the veal.

Beat egg yolk with cream. Remove veal from heat; pour egg-cream mixture over, turning veal gently to glaze all sides, and serve immediately. 6 servings.

BASIC WINE CHOICE: Fruity white

The dark, nutty flavors of a good scaloppine grow richer when tasted with a fresh and lively white wine to drink. Johannisberg Rieslings make the point perfectly, above all the one from Souverain. Dry Chenin Blancs and Fumé Blancs are rewarding alternatives.

Braised Tarragon Veal Chops

Just as truly as veal is meant for saucing, this sauce is meant for veal. Its role in that saucing is more to merge with veal and urge the meat further in the direction of sumptuousness than to counter or contrast with it.

Buttered fresh beets are a recommended vegetable.

4 shoulder veal chops, each about 8 ounces, cut 1 inch thick
About 1 tablespoon olive oil
About ¼ cup butter, divided
Salt and freshly ground black pepper to taste
¼ cup minced green onions, white part only
½ cup dry white wine
1 large clove garlic, minced or mashed
1½ teaspoons crumbled dried tarragon
¼ cup regular-strength veal or beef stock
1 tablespoon heavy cream
1 teaspoon fresh lemon juice

Wipe chops dry with a paper towel. In a large heavy skillet, heat the oil and about 2 tablespoons of the butter together over medium-high heat. Add chops, and brown on both sides. Remove chops and season well with salt and pepper.

Add 1 tablespoon more butter to skillet. Add onion, and sauté until limp. Add wine, garlic, and tarragon; cook, stirring, for a few moments to blend drippings and liquid.

Return chops to pan, and spoon juices over. Cover and simmer for about 20 minutes, or until chops are just tender; turn chops once or twice and baste occasionally during cooking. Remove chops to warm serving plates or platter.

Add stock, cream, and lemon juice to pan; cook, stirring, over high heat until liquid is blended and reduced slightly. Add the remaining 1 tablespoon butter, and gently tilt pan over heat to just melt butter (do not let butter melt down to a thin liquid). Correct seasoning with salt and pepper, and pour sauce over chops. 4 servings.

BASIC WINE CHOICE: Full, dry white

The smooth riches of a Chardonnay provide a slight but welcome contrast to the light pungency of tarragon in the dish. Pinot Blanc, Fumé Blanc, or dry Sauvignon Blanc might replace the Chardonnay. The essential thing is to drink a dry wine.

125

Avocado Veal Sauté

There is little contrast and sharpness here. This whole dish is a succession of rounded, smooth, almost voluptuous flavors: butter-browned veal, buttery avocado, mellow wine-spiced sauce. The small amount of sherry boosts the white wine flavor and adds just enough nuttiness to heighten all flavors; the total taste would be a little thinner without the sherry.

Be sure to add the avocados just before serving; otherwise, heat may alter their true flavor.

1 **cup heavy cream, divided**
4 **sirloin veal steaks, each about**
   10 ounces, cut 1 inch thick
About ¼ **cup butter, divided**
Salt and freshly ground black
   pepper to taste
½ **cup minced green onions, with**
   part of green tops
1 **cup dry white wine**
1 **tablespoon dry sherry**

1 **large clove garlic, minced**
   or mashed
2 **teaspoons fresh lemon juice**
3 **tablespoons minced fresh**
   parsley
1 **ripe avocado, pitted, peeled**
   and thinly sliced crosswise
   into arcs

Whip 3 tablespoons of the cream until stiff.

Wipe steaks dry. In a large heavy skillet over medium heat, melt about 3 tablespoons of the butter; add steaks and sauté until brown on both sides and tender, about 25 minutes total. Season generously with salt and pepper. Remove to a warm serving platter, and keep warm.

Add remaining butter to pan; add onion, and sauté until limp. Add white wine and sherry; cook over high heat until liquid reduces to about ½ cup. Add remaining cream, the garlic, and any accumulation of juice from the veal on the platter; cook and stir until liquid is reduced to consistency of heavy cream. Stir in lemon juice and parsley; correct seasoning with salt and pepper.

Arrange avocado slices over veal; sprinkle lightly with salt. Fold whipped cream into sauce, and pour over avocados and veal. 4 servings.

BASIC WINE CHOICE: Full, dry white

As with the previous recipe, Chardonnay seems the ideal wine. In fact, the two dishes together provide a short course in the subtlety of wine as accompaniment to food. With the Braised Tarragon Chops, Chardonnay provides a smooth contrast to the pungency of the herb. With the avocados and cream, Chardonnay becomes a sharp, cleansing flavor. The Chardonnays of Charles Krug and Beaulieu are styled for just these purposes.

If subtlety is not crucial, other white wines will perform the role more than adequately.

Veal Roast with White Wine

This simple treatment lets you taste the purity of good veal as veal—without clutter, and with just a subtle wine-push to enhance the meat's peak flavor.

The wine as part of the baste moistens the veal during roasting and adds a little flavor. Using some of the same wine again in the serving sauce emphasizes wine as a complementary flavor.

1 cup dry white wine, divided
¼ cup melted butter
¼ teaspoon salt
¼ teaspoon freshly ground black pepper

1 boneless veal roast (rolled shoulder or leg, not larded on the outside), about 4 pounds
½ cup regular-strength chicken broth or stock

Preheat oven to slow (325°).

Combine ⅓ cup of the wine, the butter, salt, and pepper to make a basting sauce. Place veal on rack in roasting pan. Roast for about 40 minutes per pound, or until meat thermometer registers 170°; baste frequently with basting sauce. Remove veal from oven and let stand for about 20 minutes.

Meanwhile, make serving sauce. Remove any burned drippings from roasting pan, leaving the brown drippings. Add any remaining basting sauce, the remaining wine, and the broth to drippings in pan. Heat and stir until liquid and drippings blend to a thin sauce. Taste and correct seasoning with salt and pepper.

Carve veal into thin slices, and serve with meat juices and the wine sauce over the top. 8 servings.

BASIC WINE CHOICE: Fruity white

The unadorned flavor of veal is gentle enough to make a flowery bottle of Johannisberg Riesling most refreshing. Another intriguing possibility is a tart Chenin Blanc from the new Monterey County vineyards of Mirassou or Paul Masson. Both of these—or a less costly Rhine—seem the better for being just a bit sweet.

Paprika Veal Casserole

Here, the veal, mushrooms, sour cream, and egg noodles share and exchange their richly subtle flavors to structure a quietly plush dish. The edging sweetness of paprika, onions, Worcestershire sauce, and wine sharpen those flavors—though quietly.

You can assemble this ahead and bake just in time for serving.

2 tablespoons flour
¾ teaspoon salt
½ teaspoon freshly ground black pepper
1½ pounds boneless veal stew meat, cut into ¾-inch cubes
About ¼ cup butter, divided
⅓ cup minced green onions, with part of green tops
½ pound fresh mushrooms, sliced

½ cup dry white wine
Paprika, divided
1½ cups commercial sour cream
1½ tablespoons Worcestershire sauce
4 ounces packaged dried egg noodles
½ cup sliced almonds

Combine flour, salt, and pepper in a clean paper bag; add veal, and shake to coat.

In a large heavy skillet over medium-high heat, melt about 3 tablespoons of the butter; add veal and brown (butter may also brown). Stir in onion. Add mushrooms and wine. Cover and simmer for about 30 minutes, or until veal is tender. Remove cover and cook for a few minutes more until liquid is reduced enough to just cloak veal as a sauce. Stir in 1 tablespoon paprika. Remove veal from heat, and stir in sour cream and Worcestershire.

Preheat oven to slow (325°).

Cook noodles in boiling salted water until tender; drain, and fold into veal. Correct seasoning with salt and pepper. Turn veal and noodles into a 2-quart, oiled baking dish. Melt remaining 1 tablespoon butter, toss with almonds, and sprinkle over casserole; sprinkle with a little paprika. Bake until heated through and bubbly, about 30 minutes. 4 to 6 servings.

BASIC WINE CHOICE: Fruity white

Every wise Hapsburg learned long ago to have a faintly sweet white with his veal paprika. Johannisberg Riesling is the choice for company occasions.

Oven Stew of Veal in Red Wine

2 pounds boneless veal stew
   meat, cut into 1-inch cubes
Flour
About 5 tablespoons olive oil,
   divided
Salt and freshly ground black
   pepper to taste
⅓ cup minced green onions,
   with part of green tops
¼ cup finely chopped fresh
   parsley, divided
½ pound fresh mushrooms,
   thinly sliced
1 clove garlic, minced or mashed
½ teaspoon grated fresh lemon
   peel

⅛ teaspoon crumbled dried
   sweet basil
⅛ teaspoon crumbled dried
   marjoram
⅛ teaspoon crumbled dried
   rosemary
1/16 teaspoon ground cloves
1 can (about 1 pound) peeled
   whole pear-shaped or other
   tomatoes, drained, seeded,
   and chopped
1¾ cups regular-strength
   veal stock or chicken broth
1 cup dry red wine

Preheat oven to moderate (350°).

Dust veal lightly with flour, and shake off excess. In a large skillet over moderate heat, brown veal on all sides in about 4 tablespoons of the olive oil (brown only part of the veal at a time; do not crowd in pan). Remove veal from pan and season lightly with salt and more generously with pepper.

Add remaining olive oil to pan. Add onion, and sauté until limp. Add all except 2 teaspoons of the parsley, and add remaining ingredients; cook and stir to loosen drippings.

Return veal to pan. Bake, uncovered, for 1¼ hours, or until veal is very tender and liquid is reduced to the consistency of thin sauce; stir once or twice. Sprinkle with remaining parsley before serving. 5 servings.

BASIC WINE CHOICE: Fruity red

The ingredients in this stew make the veal a background flavor but do not overwhelm its delicacy altogether. Thus, if a red wine is served with the meal it should be a light, soft Burgundy of the sort labeled Charles Krug, Louis M. Martini, or Inglenook Vintage.

129

Brandied White Veal Stew

The pair of veal stews that follows shows that it is not necessarily the kind of meat that makes the wine-with decision; it is how the meat is handled in cooking. The first is a white veal stew, light in character with white wine and gentle seasonings; a white wine goes with it. The second is a more deeply spiced stew cooked with red wine; a red wine is best to drink with it.

In both stews, the wine ingredient slowly simmers into the veal to flavor and tenderize. But in the end, you do not taste wine as wine.

In this stew you are supposed to taste a little of the brandy—hence its addition at the finish.

2 pounds boneless veal stew meat, cut into 1-inch cubes
Flour
About 5 tablespoons butter, divided
Salt and freshly ground black pepper to taste
½ cup minced green onions, white part only
1¾ cups regular-strength chicken broth or stock
1 cup dry white wine
¼ cup brandy, divided

2 tablespoons finely chopped fresh parsley, divided
1 tablespoon grated fresh lemon peel, divided
1 clove garlic, minced or mashed
1 strip (1 x 6 inches) of fresh orange zest (orange part only of orange peel)
⅛ teaspoon ground nutmeg
5 carrots, peeled and cut into julienne strips about 2 x ¼ inch
⅓ cup lightly toasted slivered almonds

Preheat oven to moderate (350°).

Dust veal lightly with flour, and shake off excess. In a large skillet over medium heat, melt about 4 tablespoons of the butter; add veal and brown on all sides (brown only part of the veal at a time; do not crowd in pan). Remove veal from pan; season lightly with salt and more generously with pepper.

Add remaining butter to pan; add onion and sauté until limp. Add broth, wine, 3 tablespoons of the brandy, 1 tablespoon of the parsley, 1 teaspoon of the lemon peel, the garlic, orange zest, and nutmeg. Cook and stir to loosen drippings.

Return veal to pan. Bake, uncovered, for 45 minutes, or until veal is tender. Add carrots, tucking them beneath liquid, and bake until carrots are tender, about 30 minutes more.

Remove orange zest. Stir in remaining brandy, parsley, and lemon peel. Taste and correct seasoning. Sprinkle with almonds. 5 servings.

BASIC WINE CHOICE: Fruity white

This stew calls for a fresh, flowery wine in the same way Veal Roast with White Wine does (see page 127). In addition to the recommendations with that recipe, try Grey Riesling from Wente, Korbel, or Sonoma Vineyards (Windsor).

13

Lamb

The rich, almost sweet, flavor of lamb is lamb's alone. Genuine devotees of lamb love it best roasted without adornment. However, even these purists admire the marinades and sauces that complicate lamb's natural flavor without submerging it. At the base of most such preparations is wine, lending an almost infallibly graceful note to the finished dishes.

Lamb, being a young animal, is naturally tender the year around. Almost any cut can be roasted, broiled, and sautéed.

The rich flavor of lamb mates perfectly with the velvety flavors of old, old wine. Connoisseurs of clarets, in fact, frequently choose roast lamb as the foil to rare bottles of claret of great age. The Basque shepherds of America's mountainous West have a similar fondness for lamb but no facilities for carting around ancient wine. Instead, they choose young red wines that have some trace of velvet—or at least velveteen.

Whatever its age, wine must be "winy" to get along with lamb—that is, it must taste strongly of both grape and alcohol. It is possible, as one recipe in this chapter demonstrates, to have a white wine with lamb, but the usual choice is a rich red—for both cooking and drinking.

A Springtime Lamb Niçoise

Braised meat and springlike flavors seldom go together, but they do in this stew. The sweet taste of onions and the fresh one of carrots give lilt to this dish from the south of France, where the celebration of spring takes place mostly in the kitchen. Olive oil is also an important flavor in the stew.

Boiled small new potatoes are an essential accompaniment to the lamb and wine-vegetable sauce. Fresh green beans might be the other side dish.

6 round-bone or shoulder lamb chops, each about 1 inch thick (about 3½ pounds total)
Salt and freshly ground black pepper to taste
1 can (15 ounces) tomato sauce
1 can (6 ounces) tomato paste
1 cup dry white wine
1 tablespoon olive oil

3 large cloves garlic, minced or mashed
About 1/16 teaspoon ground cloves
2 large sweet onions, finely chopped
4 large carrots, peeled and thinly sliced

134

Wipe chops dry. In a large heavy kettle or Dutch oven over medium heat, brown chops well on both sides in their own fat. Remove any excess fat from kettle. Season chops generously with salt and pepper.

Stir together tomato sauce, tomato paste, wine, oil, garlic, and cloves; pour over chops. Cover kettle and simmer for 30 minutes. Stir in onion and carrots. Cover again and simmer for 1 hour more, or until chops are tender. Taste juices and correct seasoning. Serve chops with juices ladled over. 6 servings.

BASIC WINE CHOICE: Fruity red

A Niçoise calls for a frisky young red, of which California has none better than a tart, dry Zinfandel from one of its coast counties wineries. Louis M. Martini's Zinfandel leads the field for us but only by a narrow margin; other contenders are Charles Krug, Beringer, Weibel, and Mirassou.

Spoon-sliced Leg of Lamb

After braising this leg of lamb in white wine for several hours, it is so tender and full of juices that you can carve it with a spoon instead of a knife.

The recipe comes from the Lyonnais district of France. There, small onions cooked in butter are the traditional accompaniment. We also like buttered new potatoes or buttered French bread with it.

An "American leg" has the shank bone removed and the meat folded back into a pocket inside the leg.

1 **leg of lamb, about 5 to 6 pounds, prepared American style**	1½ **tablespoons tomato paste**
1 **large clove garlic, slivered**	½ **teaspoon concentrated beef extract**
2 **carrots, peeled and thinly sliced**	¼ **teaspoon salt**
1 **large onion, chopped**	¼ **teaspoon freshly ground black pepper**
1 **cup dry white wine**	**Fresh parsley sprigs**

Preheat oven to very slow (275°).

With a small sharp knife, pierce lamb in several places, and insert garlic slivers. In a heavy 6-quart kettle over medium heat, brown lamb on all sides in its own fat. Add carrots and onions, and brown lightly. Stir together wine, tomato paste, beef extract, salt, and pepper; pour over lamb. Cover tightly, and bake for 4 hours, or until meat is very tender.

Remove lamb to a platter; garnish with parsley. Strain kettle juices and skim off excess fat; reheat juices and correct seasoning with salt and pepper. Spoon-carve off lamb servings, and top with juices; pass the pepper grinder. 6 to 8 servings.

BASIC WINE CHOICE: Full, dry white

Exceptions prove rules. Here the long braising results in a gentle lamb flavor, so that a flavorful white to drink becomes more appropriate than any red. Almaden's Blanc Fumé and Wente's Sauvignon Blanc are dry enough and pungent enough to go very well with the meal.

Wine-basted Butterflied Leg of Lamb

To butterfly a leg of lamb is to bone it and leave the seam open to make a nearly flat piece of meat. A leg of lamb prepared this way by your butcher, then barbecued or oven-roasted, enables you to offer a choice of rare or well-done slices of meat to please the varying tastes of your guests (the thicker part of the meat is rare, and the thinner part well done).

If you like your lamb with garlic, do this before cooking: With a sharp knife, pierce the surface of the meat in about eight places, and insert a sliver of garlic into each hole.

1 leg of lamb, about 5 to 6 pounds (weight is before boning), butterflied	3 tablespoons fresh lemon juice
⅓ cup salad oil	3 tablespoons chopped fresh parsley
⅓ cup dry red wine	¾ teaspoon salt
¼ cup A-1® Steak Sauce	½ teaspoon freshly ground black pepper

Wipe lamb dry. Beat together remaining ingredients to make a sauce. Brush sauce generously over meat surfaces.

To barbecue: Place lamb on grill, fat side up, over medium-hot coals. Cook for about 50 minutes, basting frequently with remaining sauce and turning occasionally.

To oven-roast: Preheat oven to slow (325°). Place lamb, fat side up, on rack in roasting pan. Bake for 30 minutes, basting occasionally. Turn over, and roast for about 30 minutes, basting occasionally. Turn over, and roast for about 30 minutes more, or until meat thermometer placed in thickest part of lamb registers 140° for rare (170° for well done); baste occasionally.

To carve lamb, start at one end and cut thin slices across the grain. 8 servings.

BASIC WINE CHOICE: Full, dry red

This leg of lamb benefits from the company of Petite Sirahs from California; Concannon, Mirassou, and Souverain are favored sources. These wines have the curious combination of rich flavor and glycerine smoothness that marks many wines from the south of France, Italy, and Spain.

Barbecued Cumin Kebabs

The Middle Eastern idea of the kebab has spread around the world. But to serve a kebab as an exotic sandwich is somewhat less known outside its original home.

The sandwich is simple to make at the table. Guests tuck pieces of the barbecued lamb, plus sprigs of fresh coriander, into the pocket of buttered and warmed Arab bread. Look for Arab pocket bread in Middle Eastern and specialty food stores, and for fresh coriander in Oriental food stores (under the name Chinese parsley) or Mexican-Spanish stores (where it is known as cilantro).

Whether you decide to serve the meat conventionally or as a sandwich, garnish with fresh orange wedges. The wedges can be eaten, or the juice squeezed onto the lamb.

1 **leg of lamb, 5 to 6 pounds, boned, well trimmed with all the sinews removed, and cut into 1½-inch cubes (about 3½ pounds boneless meat)**
1 **large onion, finely chopped**
1 **cup dry red wine**
½ **cup orange juice**
3 **tablespoons brown sugar**
3 **tablespoons olive oil**
1 **tablespoon chili powder**

1½ **teaspoons salt**
1 **teaspoon ground cumin**
1 **teaspoon crumbled dried oregano**
¼ **teaspoon freshly ground black pepper**
½ **teaspoon grated fresh orange peel**
1 **clove garlic, minced or mashed**

137

Put lamb cubes into a bowl. Stir together remaining ingredients to make a marinade, and pour over lamb; turn to mix thoroughly. Cover and chill for 24 hours.

Before cooking, bring lamb to room temperature. Impale cubes onto skewers. Broil over hot charcoal until browned on both sides and cooked to desired doneness (about 10 minutes total for rare); baste occasionally with marinade. Serve on or off skewers. 6 servings.

BASIC WINE CHOICE: Full, dry red

A good Barbera has a kind of sharpness about it that makes it an ideal choice to drink with a pungent spice such as cumin and a pungent leafy herb such as coriander. Petite Sirahs and Zinfandels are also possibilities.

Marinated Lamb Steaks, Charcoal-broiled

Wine in a marinade does fade into the background, but not so far that it does not provide a hint of what wine to drink with the meal, as this recipe demonstrates so well.

Both the wine and the Worcestershire sauce in the marinade help to tenderize the steaks.

Serve each steak with fresh pineapple spears and a bunch of fresh watercress or mint alongside.

4 sirloin lamb steaks, cut 1 inch thick, each about ½ pound
½ cup Worcestershire sauce
¼ cup dry red wine

¼ cup olive oil
Salt and freshly ground black pepper to taste

Wipe lamb dry and place in a bowl. Stir together Worcestershire, wine, and oil, and pour over lamb; turn lamb to coat well with marinade. Cover and chill for 24 to 48 hours; turn once.

Before cooking, bring lamb to room temperature. Place lamb on grill over hot coals and broil; turn once, and baste occasionally with marinade. When desired doneness is reached (about 15 minutes total for rare; or make a small cut in meat to check doneness), season lamb with salt and pepper. 4 servings.

BASIC WINE CHOICE: Full, dry red

As with the butterflied leg of lamb (page 136), a Petite Sirah provides the perfect balance between the sharp flavors of alcohol and the smooth ones of glycerine. This contrast parallels the strong yet sweet flavors of the lamb itself.

138

Basque Baked Lamb Shanks

The versatile role of wine as a source of both flavor and moisture is summed up in this recipe, as well as in the preceding one for lamb steaks. With the steaks, wine disappears into the marinade almost completely, resulting in a more subtle influence. With these shanks, wine is added late in the cooking process, so that it remains an important seasoning in the sauce.

Well-seasoned baked rice or white dry beans is an appropriate side dish.

4 lamb shanks
Salt and freshly ground black
   pepper to taste
Flour
1 cup dry red wine
1 tablespoon grated onion
3 tablespoons finely chopped
   fresh parsley
1 large clove garlic, minced
   or mashed

¼ teaspoon grated fresh lemon
   peel
1 tablespoon fresh lemon juice
½ teaspoon crumbled dried
   mixed herbs
¾ teaspoon salt
¼ teaspoon freshly ground
   black pepper

139

Preheat oven to moderate (350°).

Wipe shanks dry. Season generously with salt and pepper; coat with flour and shake off excess. Place in an oiled baking pan. Cover tightly and bake until shanks are tender, about 2 hours. Drain off excess fat.

Stir together remaining ingredients, and pour over shanks. Cover and bake in a hot oven (400°) for 30 minutes more. Serve with pan juices spooned over. 4 servings.

BASIC WINE CHOICE: Full, dry red

Once again Barbera and Petite Sirah are excellent wines to drink. So are Zinfandels or Burgundies from the Central Valley. The latter, in fact, are the most likely wines to find their way into a Basque shepherd's *bota*.

14

Pork

Pork is something of a culinary curiosity. The meat has a rich flavor but an indistinct one. Plain pork is much the better for a sharp seasoning with black pepper or herbs. The smokehouse and the spice shelf give other variety and dimension.

Unfortunately, these techniques for defining and improving the character of pork have an unwanted side effect: They dry the meat. Wine, as an ingredient, is an excellent restorer of moisture to pork when used as a baste or sauce.

However much care goes into the preparation, pork is to gastronomy what Norman Rockwell is to painting: a homey pleasure. The wines that are drunk with pork reflect that quality. We cannot recall a single example of a wine maker or a connoisseur bringing a memorable bottle from his cellar to serve with pork. Rather, he picks out a sturdy, agreeable wine and sits down to eat without great formality.

The recipes in this chapter encourage you to follow the winemaster's example—taking pleasure from something that is good because it is comfortable.

Wine-glazed Spareribs

In his restaurants, Trader Vic Bergeron makes one exception to the always-fresh rule: He freezes and then thaws spareribs before cooking them. He says that his Polynesian ribs are more tender this way. It may only be a part of the Trader's mystique, but both Polynesian-style ribs and these wine-glazed ribs have turned out tastier and tenderer for having been frozen.

The wine in the ingredients keeps the glaze richly flavorful at the same time that it serves as the chief moistening agent.

Spinach with toasted sesame seeds is a good accompanying vegetable.

1 **side pork spareribs, about 3 pounds, cracked in half lengthwise and to separate end ribs**	½ **cup dry red wine**
	½ **cup honey**
	2 **tablespoons wine vinegar**
	3 **tablespoons grated or minced onions**
Salt and freshly ground black pepper to taste	1 **clove garlic, minced or mashed**
1 **can (8 ounces) tomato sauce**	½ **teaspoon Worcestershire sauce**

142

Preheat oven to hot (400°).

Sprinkle spareribs generously on both sides with salt and pepper. Place in a shallow roasting pan, and bake for 45 minutes. Drain off accumulated fat.

Mix together remaining ingredients, and pour over spareribs. Reduce oven temperature to 350°, and bake ribs for 40 minutes more, or until tender; turn once, and baste occasionally during baking. Cut into serving-size pieces. 3 to 4 servings.

BASIC WINE CHOICE: Fruity red

An Italian grape called Grignolino yields the perfect wine for this dish—light, almost piquantly refreshing. A Zinfandel from California's coast counties would also be a fine choice.

It does not betray wine to say that these ribs go well with cold beer.

Braised Mustard Chops

This recipe exemplifies nearly perfectly Angelo Pellegrini's great dictum that water, by its very nature, waters everything it touches while wine does something positive for a flavor. Neither the wine nor the mustard can be identified as flavors in this dish, yet both quietly enhance the taste of pork. As a braising liquid, the wine moistens the meat and forms a natural sauce during baking.

About ¼ cup soft butter
About 1½ teaspoons salt
2 teaspoons dry mustard
½ teaspoon freshly ground
  black pepper
4 double-thick loin pork chops, each
  cut about 2¼ inches thick and with
  a pocket for stuffing

2 cups finely chopped onions
⅔ cup dry white wine
2 tablespoons finely chopped
  fresh parsley

Preheat oven to slow (325°).

Stir together butter, salt, mustard, and pepper to form a paste; rub over surfaces and inside pockets of chops. In a large heavy oven-proof skillet, over medium heat, brown chops well on both sides; remove chops. Add onion to pan, and sauté until well browned (if necessary, add a little more butter).

Spoon part of the onion into chop pockets; close openings with toothpicks. Return chops to skillet, top with remaining onion, and add wine. Cover tightly, and bake for 1½ hours, or until very tender. If necessary, add a little more wine to keep chops very moist during cooking.

Serve chops with pan juices spooned over. Sprinkle with parsley. 4 servings.

BASIC WINE CHOICE: Fruity red

Gamay and Gamay Beaujolais get along very well with pork. The younger and fresher they are, the better they mate.

If you would rather have a white wine, Johannisberg Riesling would be appropriate.

Pork Pruneaux

Sometimes exaggeration works better than subtlety. People in basement apartments sometimes paint the water pipes gaudy pink instead of the same color as the wall. Similarly, it is sometimes worthwhile to smother rich pork chops in an even richer sauce.

Wine's functions in this dish are to let the prunes become a part of the sauce, to insure juiciness in the pork, and to awaken subtle flavors in both sauce and meat.

Garnish the plates with watercress sprigs.

$1\frac{1}{2}$ **cups dry white wine**
20 pitted prunes
 4 center-cut pork loin chops, cut about 1 inch thick, then boned, trimmed, and tied (about 6 ounces each)

Salt and freshly ground black pepper to taste
About 1 tablespoon butter
1 cup heavy cream
4 teaspoons red currant jelly
1 tablespoon fresh lemon juice

Heat wine but do not boil; pour over prunes and let stand for about 2 hours.

Rub pork chops with salt and pepper to season very generously. In a large heavy skillet over medium heat, melt butter; add chops and brown well on both sides. Remove from pan.

Pour wine off prunes and into pan. Cook wine over high heat, stirring, until reduced to about $\frac{1}{2}$ cup; reduce heat.

Return chops to pan, cover tightly, and simmer for 40 minutes, or until tender; turn once. Remove chops to warm serving platter or individual plates; remove strings, and keep warm.

Add cream and jelly to pan and cook over high heat, stirring, until jelly melts and liquid is reduced to a thin sauce consistency. Add lemon juice and prunes and heat through. Taste and correct seasoning with salt and pepper. Spoon sauce and prunes over pork chops. 4 servings.

BASIC WINE CHOICE: Full, dry white

The duty of wine here is to cleanse the palate of the richness of the pork and prune combination. Wente's Sauvignon Blanc is dry and sharp enough to do the trick. A dry Zinfandel such as Louis M. Martini's is a good red wine for the same reason.

Sage Roasted Pork

Here a simple, natural wine sauce moistens the carved slices of roast pork and points up the sage-pork flavors. In short, this dish is very nearly the philosophical opposite of the preceding Pork Pruneaux.

1 boneless loin pork roast, about 3 to 5 pounds	Crumbled dried sage
Salt and freshly ground black pepper to taste	About 2 cloves garlic, slivered
	Dry white wine

Preheat oven to slow (325°).

With a sharp knife, pierce surface of pork about 1½ inches deep in about 6 to 10 places. With forefinger, press into each hole about 1/16 teaspoon *each* salt, pepper, and sage, and about ¼ clove garlic. Rub surface of pork with enough wine to moisten and with more salt, pepper, and sage. Place pork on rack in roasting pan, and bake for about 40 minutes per pound, or until meat thermometer registers about 185°. Let stand for about 15 minutes.

Remove from roasting pan all fat and any burned drippings; leave crusty brown drippings. Add ⅔ to 1 cup wine, stir to loosen drippings, and cook and stir over high heat just to blend; pour into sauce or gravy dish. Carve pork into thin slices, and pass wine sauce to ladle over. 6 to 10 servings.

145

BASIC WINE CHOICE: Fruity red

A brisk piquant young red harmonizes perfectly with the muted, almost somber, taste of sage. One of the dry Zinfandels from California's Napa Valley or Sonoma County would be a satisfactory choice. Perhaps the best choice is a Grignolino, but it is hard to find.

French Sausages in Mustard-Wine Sauce

This sausage dish originated in the Burgundy district of France where the wonderful pork sausages are a specialty, where Dijon mustard is produced, and where wine is king. The French use white wine as a sausage ingredient and as part of the sausage saucing.

Serve these sausages for supper with French bread and a crisp green salad.

1½ pounds French fresh pork-garlic sausages	2 tablespoons finely chopped fresh parsley
¼ cup butter, divided	1½ teaspoons snipped chives
1 cup dry white wine	Salt and freshly ground black
1 teaspoon Dijon-style mustard	pepper to taste

Place sausages in a large heavy skillet with cold water to almost cover. Simmer, covered, for 15 minutes. Drain sausages and dry with paper towels.

In same skillet melt about 1 tablespoon of the butter and brown sausages on all sides over medium heat. Remove sausages to warm serving plates or platter and keep warm.

Remove any excess fat from skillet; retain the crusty drippings. Add rest of butter to skillet, and cook over medium-high heat until it foams and browns. Add wine and cook over high heat, stirring, until liquid is reduced to a thin sauce consistency. Remove from heat and whisk in mustard, parsley, chives, a small amount of salt, and a generous amount of pepper to taste. Pour over sausages. 4 servings.

BASIC WINE CHOICE: Fruity red

No one in the United States has figured out how to make a wine as light-hearted as the Beaujolais that goes into carafes in the restaurants of Burgundy. But Gamay from California comes close enough to quench a great country dinner of sausages.

Wine-glazed Ham Steak

Wine and apricots shape a gentle glaze for a baking ham, a departure from the more usual spicy sharp cloakings.

In this recipe, you should cook with the wine you choose to drink: If you want to drink a rosé, cook with it; if you drink a white, cook with a white.

1 2-inch-thick fully cooked smoked ham steak, about 3 pounds Whole cloves Medium-dry white or rosé wine	1 can (1 pound) whole or halved apricots 2 tablespoons honey 1 teaspoon dry mustard

Preheat oven to moderate (375°).

Wipe ham dry with a damp cloth. Diagonally slash fat about every 2 inches; insert about 3 cloves in each slash. Place ham in a shallow baking pan, and add wine to reach about ½ inch up the ham. Cover pan, and bake for 1 hour. Drain baking juices off ham and discard.

Drain syrup from apricots into a saucepan; boil until reduced to about ⅓ cup. Stir in honey, mustard, and 1 tablespoon wine. Arrange apricots decoratively over top and alongside ham; center each with a clove. Spoon syrup mixture over all. Bake, uncovered, for 15 minutes more or until glazed; baste once or twice.

Slice ham and serve with pan juices and apricots. 6 to 8 servings.

BASIC WINE CHOICE: Rosé or fruity white

Ham defies serious wine even more than other pork. Any fresh, fruity rosé slakes the thirst brought on by ham's salt and smoke. For those who prefer white wine, a Chenin Blanc or Rhine will serve admirably. At a festive summertime meal, an extra dry or sec champagne would be appropriate.

147

Sherried Ham Slices

This recipe has been popular in the western part of the United States for many years—probably because it is so easy to make and because of the natural abundance of California walnuts and California sherry.

3 tablespoons light brown sugar
1 tablespoon fresh lemon juice
2 smoked ham slices (with or without bone), each ¾ to 1 pound

¾ cup chopped walnuts
¼ cup butter, divided
¾ cup dry sherry, divided

Mix brown sugar and lemon juice, and rub over both sides of ham slices; allow to stand for 15 minutes. In a small pan, sauté walnuts in 2 tablespoons of the butter until lightly toasted.

Melt rest of butter in a large heavy skillet over medium-high heat; add ham slices, and brown on both sides (sugar should caramelize slightly). Add 1 cup boiling water and ½ cup of the sherry. Simmer slowly, uncovered, until ham is tender and juices reduce to a very thin syrup, about 45 minutes; turn ham once.

Top ham with walnuts. Pour on remaining sherry and heat through. Cut ham into serving-size pieces, and top each serving with walnuts and pan juices. 5 to 6 servings.

BASIC WINE CHOICE: Rosé or fruity white

A ham is a ham is a ham. Drink rosé.

148

Red Wine Meat Sauce for Pasta or Polenta, p. 119

15

Desserts

Most desserts are very flexible in the face of season and circumstance. The same recipe can go forth unchanged on a summer afternoon, a wintry late evening, or as the capper to a fine dinner.

What is more, having guests in for dessert is simpler and less costly for a hostess than having them in for dinner, so it provides an opportunity to entertain more often than might otherwise be possible.

Wine, in its myriad forms, increases the potential enormously. The only problem is avoiding an embarrassment of riches.

A sweet wine served at the end of a meal is very nearly the dessert itself and requires little or no other sweet. A wintertime classic is a good port and a plate of cheeses, the ultimate pairing being an old port and an old Stilton cheese with a few water biscuits. In summer, a sweet white wine, such as a cool sweet sauterne, can be paired with some fresh ripe fruit—perhaps a bowl of strawberries.

Nearly all the desserts in this chapter fall in the sweet category. Most of them are rich enough to stand alone as a party's focal point—either at midday or in the evening. All are suitable for rounding out a meal.

If you serve these desserts after dinner, you probably will prefer coffee to wine as a beverage. If you have them alone, let the season be your guide as to the choice of wine. When the weather is warm and sunny, stay with sweet white wines of 11 or 12 percent alcohol. In the cold months, try one of the higher-alcohol wines. Dessert wines are described in detail on pages 32-33.

Champagne Peaches
152

Pears Baked in Red Wine
152

Strawberries and Port
153

Port-spiced Fruits in Compote
153

Ported Blueberries Sundae
154

Ruby Raspberry Ice
154

Brandied Apricot Cream
155

Cream Cheese Shortbreads with Brandy Almond Glaze
155

Deep-dish Apple Pie, Sauterne
156

Orange-Pecan Crêpes, Brandy Flamed
157

A Sherry Trifle
159

Mince Muscat Crisp
160

Pecan-Brandy Date Cake with Brandied Hard Sauce
160

Brandied Vanilla Cream Coffee
162

Zabaglione
162

Champagne Peaches

The ancient, honorable idea behind Champagne Peaches is frothy fun. Certainly, it does not honor champagne with any great reverence. Use a dessert champagne—an extra dry or sec—so that you can fill each glass with a few extra sips to prolong the pleasure. To add extra whimsy, garnish each serving with a few candied blossoms of violets or roses.

Large halves of peaches
    (poached fresh peaches or
    canned peaches, drained),
    chilled

Extra-dry or sec champagne,
    chilled
Candied flower blossoms
    (optional)

For *each* serving, place a peach half, cut side up, in a wide-bowled, stemmed wine or champagne glass. Pour on enough champagne to cover. Garnish with candied blossoms. Eat the peach with a spoon; then sip champagne.

152

Pears Baked in Red Wine

The wine poaches the pears, even as it cooks down slightly to a syrup, and gives the finished dish a refreshingly tart edge.

6 fresh pears with stems,
    unpeeled
6 whole cloves

1½ cups dry red wine
¾ cup firmly packed
    brown sugar

Preheat oven to hot (400°).

Pierce blossom end of each pear with a clove. Place pears on sides in a deep baking dish. Combine wine, sugar, and ¾ cup water, and pour over pears (syrup need not cover pears).

Cover and bake for 30 minutes, basting or very gently turning pears occasionally. Uncover and continue baking, basting once or twice, for 15 minutes more, or until pears are tender when pierced with a toothpick. Serve hot or cold in wine syrup. 6 servings.

Strawberries and Port

In this recipe, the wine is a direct sauce and seasoning, added just before serving.

Sugar the strawberries with some judgment, according to the berries' need for added sweetness and according to the sweetness of your port. You can serve crisp wafer cookies alongside.

1 pint fresh strawberries
Sugar

About ¼ cup ruby port

Rinse and stem strawberries, and slice them into a bowl. Sprinkle with sugar to sweeten, and gently turn. Chill for about 1 hour. Spoon berries into 4 stemmed dessert glasses. Pour about 1 tablespoon port over each serving. 4 servings.

153

Port-spiced Fruits in Compote

This dish is a deeply satisfying dessert by itself, but if you want a luxurious finish, serve it with heavy cream or softly whipped unsweetened cream.

1 cup (about 6 ounces) moist
**   dried apricots**
1 cup moist dried prunes,
**   pitted or with pits**
3 tablespoons golden raisins

½ cup ruby port
⅓ cup firmly packed
**   brown sugar**
4 thin lemon slices
⅛ teaspoon ground nutmeg

Cook apricots, prunes, and raisins separately in water to cover until tender. Drain off cooking liquid from each fruit, reserving 1 cup of the combined liquids. Put fruits into a pretty serving bowl.

Combine the reserved liquid with the port, sugar, lemon slices, and nutmeg in a saucepan, and slowly heat until sugar melts; do not boil. Pour over fruits. Cover and chill for 12 to 24 hours. 6 servings.

Ported Blueberries Sundae

The affinity of port for dairy products does not stop with cheeses. Combined with fruit, port makes an intriguingly complex topping for ice cream.

Be sure the ice cream is frozen hard. You may wish to dip out scoop-servings ahead of time and freeze them firm on a chilled baking sheet.

1½ cups ruby or tawny port
6 tablespoons firmly packed brown sugar
¾ teaspoon grated fresh lemon peel

1 cup blueberries, fresh or thawed frozen
6 large scoops rich vanilla ice cream

Combine port, sugar, and lemon peel in a saucepan and heat slowly, stirring, until sugar dissolves. Add blueberries and heat through. Place a scoop of ice cream into each of 6 stemmed dessert glasses. Ladle warm sauce over and serve immediately. 6 servings.

154

Ruby Raspberry Ice

This is denser in effect than are most ices and also more deeply flavored. Serve the ice alone with simple crisp cookies, or serve it in tandem with rich vanilla ice cream—a scoop of each for a serving.

1 package (10 ounces) frozen raspberries in syrup
¼ cup sugar
Few grains of salt
1 teaspoon grated fresh lemon peel

1 tablespoon fresh lemon juice
¼ teaspoon grated fresh orange peel
½ cup fresh orange juice
2 to 3 tablespoons ruby port

Combine raspberries, ½ cup water, and sugar in a saucepan. Heat to boiling; then simmer for about 6 minutes. Press through a sieve so as to strain out seeds and purée the berries; cool resulting purée and juices.

Stir in remaining ingredients. Freeze until mushy. Beat with electric mixer. Spread in a chilled freezing tray, and freeze until firm. Cover to store. 4 servings.

Brandied Apricot Cream

Brandy magnifies the rich, deep-fruited flavor of dried apricots. In this recipe, brandy adds the best of its qualities because it is not altered by cooking, so it is not a waste to use a smooth, fine brandy. The amount called for is small enough that the proprietor of the bottle should not complain. Much.

1 cup (about 6 ounces) dried apricots	1 cup sifted powdered sugar
⅓ cup brandy	½ teaspoon vanilla extract
1 teaspoon fresh lemon juice	Few grains of salt
1 cup heavy cream	½ cup finely chopped walnuts
2 egg yolks	Curls or gratings of unsweetened chocolate

Gently boil apricots in a saucepan with water to cover until very tender; drain. While hot, stir apricots vigorously with a fork or slotted spoon to make a rough purée; cool thoroughly. Stir in brandy and lemon juice.

In a large bowl, whip the cream. In another bowl, beat egg yolks with powdered sugar, vanilla, and salt until smooth and thick; fold into whipped cream along with cooled apricot purée and walnuts.

Spoon into stemmed dessert glasses, and chill for 2 to 24 hours. Before serving, sprinkle lightly with chocolate. 8 servings.

155

Cream Cheese Shortbreads

This recipe demonstrates how the wine ingredient—brandy—can be a baking glaze in a dessert. Here the brandy bakes into and onto the cheese shortbread.

The subtle, salty tang of cheese in the cookie base provides a pleasant counterpoint flavor to the sweet-sharp brandy-almond glaze. Hot tea or coffee with the dessert brings out the contrast best, though a sweet sauterne does the trick very well, too.

10 tablespoons soft butter	¼ teaspoon salt
6 tablespoons sugar	1½ cups sifted flour
4 ounces soft cream cheese	Brandy-Almond Glaze (recipe follows)
1¼ teaspoons vanilla extract	

Preheat oven to moderate (350°).

In a mixing bowl, beat butter, sugar, cheese, vanilla, and salt together until smooth. Add flour, and stir with a spoon until well blended. With back of a spoon, spread mixture over bottom of an oiled 9- x 13-inch baking pan; press smooth with lightly floured fingertips. Bake for 25 to 30 minutes, or until lightly browned. Cool on a rack.

Spoon Brandy-Almond Glaze evenly over cookie base. Return to oven and bake for 20 to 25 minutes more, or until deep golden. Cool on a rack. Cut into 48 slender bars.

Brandy-Almond Glaze

½ cup butter	2 tablespoons honey
¼ cup sugar	¾ teaspoon almond extract
¼ cup brandy	1 cup sliced almonds

Combine all ingredients in a saucepan, and heat to a full rolling boil; boil for 1 minute, stirring. Remove from heat to cool slightly.

Deep-dish Apple Pie, Sauterne

In Germany, an evening invitation for dessert most likely means a cake-type dessert and some chilled sweet white wine, then coffee. The effect is elegant. This recipe takes to a sweet sauterne or a light Muscat *and* satisfies the American passion for pie.

Resist any temptation to increase the amounts of spices in this recipe, as any more spice will overwhelm the subtle balance of wine and spice. The unsweetened whipped cream is important; without it the pie is just a touch too sweet.

⅔ cup sugar	2 tablespoons sweet sauterne or light muscat
1½ tablespoons flour	
¼ teaspoon ground cinnamon	1 teaspoon fresh lemon juice
¼ teaspoon ground nutmeg	1 cup sifted flour
Pinch of ground cloves	2 tablespoons sugar
½ teaspoon salt, divided	6 tablespoons butter
6 tart cooking apples, peeled, cored, and thinly sliced	1 egg, beaten
	1½ to 2 cups heavy cream, softly whipped
	Sugar

Preheat oven to very hot (450°).
Stir together the ⅔ cup sugar, 1½ tablespoons flour, cinnamon, nutmeg,

cloves, and ⅜ teaspoon of the salt. Gently mix with apples. Add wine and lemon juice, and gently mix. Spread over bottom of a shallow 2½-quart baking dish.

Sift together into a mixing bowl the 1 cup flour, 2 tablespoons sugar, and the remaining ⅛ teaspoon salt. Cut in butter until particles are fine. Add half the beaten egg, and toss with a fork to mix. Gather dough into a ball; on a lightly floured board, roll it out to fit top of baking dish. Arrange pastry over apples, cut with a decorative vent, and flute at edges to seal; brush with remaining egg, and sprinkle lightly with sugar.

Bake pie for 10 minutes; reduce heat to moderate (350°), and bake for 40 minutes more or until deep golden. Cool until warm. Spoon out pie servings, and top with whipped cream. 8 servings.

Orange-Pecan Crêpes, Brandy-flamed

Flaming desserts have an irresistibly dramatic allure. Brandy is the tastiest fuel for such a fire. This recipe also gives you a good chance to taste the marked flavor change that results from burning a brandy.

When cooks have trouble getting a dish to flame, it is usually because the brandy is not warm. The secret is to heat the brandy—gently, so as not to evaporate the alcohol—before attempting to ignite it. As soon as the first small, blue flame appears, begin spooning the liquid up to let air get to it; the more you aerate with spooning, the more intense and durable your flame. Also, do not dilute the brandy with other ingredients until the flaming is over, as dilution obviously cuts down on the fire.

⅓ cup butter
½ cup sugar
Grated peel of 1 orange
¼ cup fresh orange juice
2 teaspoons fresh lemon juice
⅛ teaspoon ground cinnamon

8 Crêpes (recipe follows)
¼ cup brandy
¼ cup finely chopped lightly toasted pecans
Whipped Cream (recipe follows)

In a large chafing dish set over medium-low flame (or in a large skillet over medium-low heat), melt butter. Stir in the sugar, orange peel, orange juice, lemon juice, and cinnamon; stir until sugar melts.

Fold each crêpe in half twice to make a quarter-circle shape. Place crêpes in chafing dish, and spoon syrup over them. Add brandy at edge of chafing dish, and as soon as it warms, light it. Spoon flaming syrup over crêpes, lifting it high to allow air to reach it.

When flames die, arrange 2 crêpes, slightly overlapping, on each dessert plate. Spoon syrup over, sprinkle with pecans, and put a spoonful of Whipped Cream alongside. 4 servings.

Crêpes

3 eggs	1 cup milk
6 tablespoons flour	Butter
⅜ teaspoon salt	

In bowl, beat eggs slightly; add flour and salt, and beat until smooth. Gradually add milk, and beat until batter is smooth. Cover, and chill for 30 minutes to 1 hour; stir to blend well before using.

To make *each* crêpe, heat about ½ teaspoon of the butter over medium-high heat in a 7- or 8-inch crêpe pan. Pour in about 3 tablespoons of the batter; quickly tilt and rotate the pan so batter covers bottom of pan. When lightly brown on bottom, turn over crêpe and lightly brown other side. Slip crêpe onto a clean towel. About 12 crêpes.

158

Whipped Cream

¾ cup heavy cream	¾ teaspoon vanilla extract
1 tablespoon sugar	

Beat cream with sugar and vanilla until softly whipped.

A Sherry Trifle

Here the wine becomes much of the saucing and much of the seasoning.

Since the ingredients are all cool when the wine is added, the wine does not change its composition or taste.

1 8- or 9-inch round sponge-cake layer, about 6 ounces
6 tablespoons cream sherry, divided
About ¾ pound crisp almond macaroons
2 cans (1 pound 14 ounces each) peeled whole apricots, drained, halved, and pitted

Coffee Custard Sauce (recipe follows)
1 cup heavy cream
1 tablespoon sugar
½ teaspoon vanilla extract
3 tablespoons lightly toasted sliced almonds

Place cake layer in bottom of a 2½- to 3-quart handsome crystal serving bowl; sprinkle evenly with 4 tablespoons of the sherry. Arrange half the macaroons over cake, and sprinkle with 1 tablespoon of the sherry. Arrange half the apricots over macaroons; top apricots with remaining macaroons, and sprinkle with the remaining tablespoon of sherry. Place rest of apricots over top layer of macaroons, and pour cooled custard sauce evenly over all. Cover and chill for 4 to 24 hours.

At serving time, softly whip the cream with sugar and vanilla, and swirl over top of trifle; sprinkle with almonds. Spoon out to serve. 10 to 12 servings.

Coffee Custard Sauce

4 egg yolks
2 cups dairy half-and-half (light cream)
¼ cup sugar
⅛ teaspoon salt

1½ teaspoons instant coffee powder (or instant coffee crystals crushed to a powder)
½ teaspoon vanilla extract

In top part of a double boiler, beat together thoroughly the egg yolks, half-and-half, sugar, and salt. Cook over hot (not boiling) water, stirring, until mixture thickens slightly and coats a silver spoon. Remove from heat. Strain.

Stir in coffee and vanilla. Allow to cool, stirring occasionally.

159

Mince Muscat Crisp

The richness of this crisp is caused almost more by the deep, sweet spiciness of the fruit than by the sugar-crumb topping.

4 cups peeled and sliced tart cooking apples
1½ cups prepared mincemeat
⅓ cup Muscatel
1 cup flour
⅔ cup firmly packed brown sugar

½ teaspoon salt
½ teaspoon ground cinnamon
½ teaspoon ground nutmeg
6 tablespoons butter
1½ cups heavy cream, softly whipped

Preheat oven to moderate (375°).

Mix apples, mincemeat, and Muscatel. Turn into an 8-inch square baking pan.

Combine flour, sugar, salt, cinnamon, and nutmeg. Cut in butter until mixture is crumbly. Sprinkle evenly over fruit.

Bake for 40 to 45 minutes, or until topping is rich golden brown. Serve while warm with whipped cream. 6 to 8 servings.

Pecan-Brandy Date Cake

Brandy in this cake enhances and blends flavors. Brandy in a hard sauce provides a completing, smoothing effect.

If at all possible, bake the cake a day ahead of serving, cool it, and cover it; then reheat in the oven before serving. The cake is better for at least one day's aging; in fact, it seems to get even richer and more moist up to a full week after baking.

You could sip brandy with this dessert or add a little brandy to accompanying strong black coffee or simply let the brandy in the cake suffice for your supply of dessert brandy, and serve plain hot coffee with the cake.

1 cup pitted dates, cut up
1 teaspoon baking soda
½ cup butter
¼ cup brandy
1 egg
½ cup sugar
1 teaspoon vanilla extract

1½ cups sifted all-purpose flour
1 teaspoon baking powder
½ cup chopped pecans
About 2 cups sliced fresh strawberries
Brandied Brown-Sugar Hard Sauce (recipe follows)

Preheat oven to moderate (350°).

In a large mixing bowl, toss dates with soda. Add ¾ cups boiling water and butter, and stir until butter is melted; stir in brandy. Set aside to cool to lukewarm.

In a small bowl, beat egg well with sugar and vanilla; stir into cooled date mixture. Sift flour with baking powder into date mixture; stir to mix well. Stir in pecans. Turn into an oiled 9-inch square baking pan.

Bake for about 35 minutes, or until toothpick inserted in center comes out clean. Cool on a rack. Reheat to warm before serving.

Cut into squares or rectangles, and top each serving with a spoonful of hard sauce and a heaping spoonful of strawberries. 10 servings.

Brandied Brown-Sugar Hard Sauce

⅔ cup soft butter	2 egg yolks
2 cups firmly packed light brown sugar	2 to 3 tablespoons brandy

Beat together butter, sugar, and egg yolks until light and fluffy. Beat in the brandy.

NOTE: When fresh strawberries are out of season, there is an alternate version of this cake. Instead of topping cake with strawberries and the hard sauce, you can bake the cake with a finishing of pecan panocha and top it with whipped cream. In order to do this, make the following changes in the recipe.

Leave out the ½ cup chopped pecans. Bake cake for only 25 minutes. Then stir together and gently spread this topping over cake: 1 cup firmly packed brown sugar; 1 cup chopped pecans; 3 tablespoons melted butter; 3 tablespoons heavy cream. Bake cake for 10 to 15 minutes more, or until topping is golden brown. Serve warm, topped generously with unsweetened, softly whipped cream (about 1¾ cups heavy cream measured before whipping). Or simply serve the cake unadorned, cut into 1-inch squares, as small cakelike confections.

Brandied Vanilla Cream Coffee

This coffee drink can be the dessert. You don't really need more.

Split a vanilla bean, put it into an attractive decanter, and fill decanter with brandy (or just put split vanilla bean into bottle of brandy). Cover and let stand for at least one day—or indefinitely—before serving.

Softly whip heavy cream, and flavor it lightly with sugar and vanilla. For *each* serving, pour freshly brewed hot black coffee into a cup. Pass brandy and a bowl of the whipped cream and let each guest add them to coffee in the amounts he wishes.

Zabaglione

Italian in origin, Zabaglione classically calls for Italian Marsala as the wine ingredient. However, this velvety froth of egg yolks and wine has become far too widely approved over the years to appear in only its classic form. Other rich and rather sweet dessert wines—such as cream sherry or a tawny port—work wonderfully well as substitutes for the Marsala.

It isn't necessary, but a sprinkle of semi-sweet chocolate gratings or curls on top of each serving adds a surprising dimension of flavor.

A likely Marsala for the recipe or for drinking is Royal Host by East-Side Winery.

6 egg yolks   **6 tablespoons Marsala**
6 tablespoons sugar

Beat egg yolks and sugar together in top part of double boiler. Place over hot (not boiling) water and gradually beat in Marsala. Cook, beating constantly with a wire whisk or rotary beater, until thick, light, and smooth, about 5 to 10 minutes. Pour into small, stemmed glasses and serve immediately, or chill and serve cold. 4 servings.

16

Brunches and Luncheons

Brunches and luncheons are designed to allow people to spend a free day frivolously—or at least not seriously. Neither the food nor the wine requires much study or concern.

Eggs and fruit dominate the dishes in this chapter. Rosés and not-quite-dry whites are the wines to go with them. If the shadow of an excuse presents itself, have a sparkling wine instead.

In short, indulge.

Poached Eggs with Red Wine Sauce

The idea of poached eggs under a red wine sauce comes from the Burgundy region of France. This recipe simplifies the French method.

Cook one egg per person for light luncheon servings. For a supper, double the recipe and serve two eggs per person.

If you wish, you can make the sauce ahead of time and slowly reheat it before serving.

4 **round brioche or egg-bread slices, each ⅜ inch thick and 3 inches in diameter**	4 **poached eggs**
	Red Wine Sauce (recipe follows)
1½ **tablespoons butter**	**Finely chopped fresh parsley**

In skillet over medium heat, melt butter and sauté brioche slices until crisp and golden on both sides. For *each* serving, place a brioche slice on a warm plate, top it with a poached egg, spoon one-fourth of the wine sauce over, and sprinkle lightly with parsley. 4 servings.

166

NOTE: If you wish to poach eggs slightly ahead of serving time, you can hold them, warm and still soft, in the following way. Fill a shallow pan 2 inches deep with water that is hot to the touch. Trim off ragged edges of eggs, and slip eggs into pan. Place, uncovered, in a warm oven (150°) for as long as 30 minutes.

Red Wine Sauce

2 **strips bacon, diced**	3/16 **teaspoon crumbled dried thyme**
2 **teaspoons minced shallots**	
1 **tablespoon butter**	1 **small clove garlic, minced or mashed**
1 **cup dry red wine**	
1 **cup canned condensed beef consommé, undiluted**	**Freshly ground black pepper**
	2 **tablespoons soft butter**
½ **bay leaf**	1 **tablespoon flour**

Cook bacon in boiling water for 3 minutes; drain.

In wide skillet, sauté shallots in 1 tablespoon butter just to heat and coat with butter. Add bacon, wine, consommé, bay leaf, thyme, garlic, and a generous amount of pepper. Cook over high heat, stirring, until liquid is reduced to 1 cup.

Mix soft butter with flour. Remove wine mixture from heat and quickly whisk in flour mixture. Return to heat, and boil for 30 seconds, stirring. Remove bay leaf.

This is a chance to break all sorts of wine-serving rules. Seldom do you cook with red and drink white. Seldom can an egg be made into a fine accompaniment to any type of wine, but here is one of the times. Both egg and wine should be young and fresh, and the wine close to dry. The Christian Brothers' Chablis is a good beginning point.

Parmesan-Sherry Baked Eggs

These eggs are for a brunch. Serve citrus fruits for the first course and thin-sliced warm ham and toast or English muffins with the eggs. If you have hearty eaters, bake two eggs per person and add hot buttered spinach to the morning's menu.

167

8 teaspoons soft butter	2 tablespoons grated Parmesan cheese
4 teaspoons dry sherry	
4 eggs	4 teaspoons sliced almonds
Freshly ground black pepper	Finely chopped fresh parsley

Preheat oven to moderate (350°).

Prepare *each* of 4 individual small baking dishes as follows. Butter with 2 teaspoons butter. Add 1 teaspoon sherry. Break in 1 egg. Season with pepper. Sprinkle with 1½ teaspoons cheese and with 1 teaspoon almonds. Bake for 10 minutes, or just until egg begins to set and whites are milky looking but still soft (egg will continue to cook as you serve it in hot baking dish). Sprinkle generously with parsley. Serve immediately. 4 servings.

BASIC WINE CHOICE: Fruity white

Brunches and luncheons generally call for a slightly sweet drinking wine; in particular, these flavorful eggs need such a wine even more. There is no such thing as a perfect wine to go with eggs, but Almaden's Gewürztraminer, Paul Masson's Emerald Dry, and Charles Krug's or Beringer's Chenin Blanc come close enough to give real pleasure.

Wine-toasted Sauté Mushrooms

Serve these wine-glazed mushrooms with thin buttered toast points or toasted English muffin strips and a gentle salad of soft-leaf lettuce dressed lightly with oil, fresh lemon juice, salt, and pepper.

You must cook the mushrooms until they begin to brown and toast and lose their limpness.

1½ **pounds fresh mushrooms, very thinly sliced**	½ **cup butter** 1 **cup dry white wine**

In a large heavy skillet, melt butter; add mushrooms and sauté over medium-high heat, stirring occasionally, until the mushrooms are deep golden and almost toasted, the butter browns slightly, and all mushroom liquid disappears, about 20 to 30 minutes. Add wine, and continue cooking until it cooks down completely. 2 to 3 servings.

BASIC WINE CHOICE: Fruity white

The dark, earthy flavors of mushroom, heightened here by sautéed butter, mate with nothing better than an opposite—a light white wine that is as fresh and fragrant as a spring morning. We recommend Charles Krug's or Simi's Gewürztraminer, though a less expensive alternative would be a Rhine.

Almond Chicken Mousse

This is a softly molded chicken salad. If possible, you should make it a full twenty-four hours before serving in order for the flavors to be developed and mingled to their maximum.

Hot croissants or butter biscuits are good with it.

1 envelope unflavored gelatin
1 cup chicken broth
⅓ cup dry white wine
1 tablespoon scraped or very finely grated onion
About ½ teaspoon salt
About ½ teaspoon paprika
About ½ teaspoon freshly ground black pepper
About ¼ teaspoon ground nutmeg

Pinch of cayenne
1½ cups finely diced cooked chicken
½ cup ground and toasted blanched almonds
Salt and cayenne to taste
1 cup heavy cream
Toasted slivered almonds
Watercress sprigs

In top part of double boiler, sprinkle gelatin over ¼ cup cold water to soften; heat over hot water until dissolved. Stir in broth, wine, onion, salt, paprika, pepper, nutmeg, and cayenne. Chill until syrupy. Stir in chicken and ground almonds. Taste and correct seasoning to season very well with salt and cayenne. Whip cream and fold in.

Turn mixture into a lightly oiled 1½-quart mold. Cover and chill until set —at least 4 hours but preferably 24 hours. Unmold on a chilled salad platter. Border top of salad with slivered almonds; border base of salad generously with watercress. 6 servings.

NOTE: To toast almonds, sprinkle on baking sheet and lightly brown in a moderate oven (350°); stir or shake occasionally.

169

BASIC WINE CHOICE: Sparkling wine or fruity white

Smooth, plush mousses mate admirably with wines that are on the one hand a bit prickly, and on the other somewhat less than dry. An extra-dry or sec champagne would be an excellent choice; a less obvious choice would be one of the middle-of-the-road Rieslings (such as from The Christian Brothers or Paul Masson) or a Traminer (from Charles Krug or Inglenook).

Chicken á la King

The difference in the flavor of this dish when sherry wine is added to it is remarkable, though the amount is only two tablespoons. Here sherry performs as the sauce finish, yet you do not taste sherry as sherry.

3 tablespoons butter, divided
¼ cup finely chopped green bell pepper
¼ pound fresh mushrooms, thinly sliced
2 tablespoons flour
¾ teaspoon salt
2 cups dairy half-and-half (light cream)
3 cups diced cooked chicken
1 tablespoon fresh lemon juice

1 teaspoon onion juice (scraped from fresh onion)
3 egg yolks
¼ cup very soft butter
½ teaspoon paprika
1 jar (2 ounces) sliced pimientos, drained and diced
2 tablespoons dry sherry
Patty shells or toast cups
Parsley sprigs

In a large heavy skillet, melt 2 tablespoons of the butter; add green pepper and mushrooms and sauté until tender. Remove vegetables from pan. Add 1 more tablespoon butter to the skillet; add flour and salt, and stir over low heat to make a smooth paste. Gradually add half-and-half, cooking and stirring to make a smooth, slightly thickened sauce. Add chicken and heat through. Add lemon juice and onion juice, and heat to bubbling.

Meanwhile, beat together egg yolks, the ¼ cup soft butter, and paprika. Add all at once to bubbling chicken mixture, stirring until blended. Remove from heat immediately. Stir in pimientos and sherry. Serve in warmed patty shells or toast cups, and garnish with parsley. 5 to 6 servings.

BASIC WINE CHOICE: Dry or fruity white

Elevated in this recipe above its usual station, Chicken à la King is easy company for all but the sweetest of white wines. For drier tastes, a white Pinot or Chablis will serve admirably. For people who prefer a touch of sweet, a Chenin Blanc or Rhine is the answer.

Vintage Aspic

Marjorie Lumm, director of the Home Advisory Service for California's Wine Institute, has been matching California wines and California foods for years. This is her aspic recipe.

It is better when it is made a day ahead of serving; the extra chilling time gets the flavors together more completely and more fully than when the aspic is served the day it is made.

The aspic is big enough in taste and content to stand alone as a luncheon salad, in which case it serves four. But if you want to make it part of a more generous luncheon or if you want to serve it as a supper dish, extend the menu with warm ham slices and hot buttered buns. Guests can make their own small ham sandwiches, if they wish.

1¼ cups tomato juice
¼ teaspoon salt
⅛ teaspoon crumbled dried basil
1 package (3 ounces) lemon-flavored gelatin
¾ cup dry white wine
3 tablespoons white wine vinegar
⅓ cup crumbled blue cheese
Crisp lettuce leaves
1 cup commercial sour cream
About 1½ teaspoons prepared horseradish

In saucepan, heat tomato juice, salt, and basil to boiling; add gelatin, and stir until dissolved. Remove from heat; stir in wine and vinegar. Chill until mixture begins to thicken; stir in cheese.

Turn into a lightly oiled 3-cup mold, or into 4 to 6 individual small molds. Chill until set. Unmold onto chilled platter or serving plates lined with lettuce. Stir together sour cream and horseradish, and pass as a dressing. 4 servings.

BASIC WINE CHOICE: Fruity white

Combining cheese and tomato in a dish usually calls for a red wine to drink, but not in this case. Chill is one reason, and the enhanced fruitiness of the tomatoes is the other. The suitable wine would be a dry Semillon or dry sauterne.

Summer Fruit Salad Platter

This platter is probably in its ideal setting at an *al fresco* luncheon on a summer day. Since both salad and wine are cooling, you might wish to serve hot buttered yeast buns for a spot of warmth.

8 fresh plums, halved and
  pitted
8 fresh apricots, halved and
  pitted
About ¼ cup rosé wine
Tender lettuce leaves
Roll-ups of thinly sliced ham
  (optional)

Small clusters of summer
  cherries and/or seedless grapes
Red currant jelly
Almond-Cheese Whip (recipe
  follows)

Put plums and apricots into a bowl, pour wine over, and chill for about 1 hour; gently turn fruits once or twice.

At serving time, line a chilled salad platter or 4 chilled luncheon plates with lettuce. Lift fruits from wine and arrange over greens. Arrange ham alongside and garnish with cherries and/or grapes. Put a small spoonful of currant jelly in center of each apricot half. Pass Almond–Cheese Whip to spoon as a dressing over fruits and lettuce. 4 servings.

Almond-Cheese Whip

6 ounces soft cream cheese
¼ teaspoon salt
3 tablespoons rosé wine
½ teaspoon grated fresh lemon
  peel

¼ cup finely chopped toasted
  almonds

With an electric mixer, beat together cream cheese and salt until light and fluffy. Gradually add the wine, beating until mixture is soft and smooth. Fold in lemon peel and almonds.

BASIC WINE CHOICE: Rosé

Grenache and Gamay rosés strike the delicate balance between sweet and dry that is appropriate for this summery lunch.

172

Rose and Berry Molded Salad

This salad is to be served as the main luncheon dish, with ham and/or turkey slices alongside.

Place the salad on broken lettuce leaves that have been tossed with a dressing of oil, fresh lemon juice, tarragon, salt, pepper, and a pinch of sugar beaten together with a fork.

1 large package (6 ounces) black cherry-flavored gelatin
1½ cups rosé wine
1 pint fresh strawberries, washed, hulled, and halved
2 cups fresh blueberries or 1 package (10 ounces) frozen blueberries, almost thawed
4 oranges, peeled, cut into segments with all membrane removed, and the segments halved
Broken lettuce leaves with tarragon dressing

Pour 2 cups boiling water over gelatin in a bowl and stir to dissolve. Add wine and ½ cup cool water. Chill until syrupy.

Arrange some of the strawberries over the bottom of a 3-quart mold, or small individual molds, add enough of the cooled gelatin to cover berries, and chill until set. Fold remaining strawberries, the blueberries, and the oranges into remaining gelatin, and turn into mold. Chill until set.

173

At serving time, unmold onto a chilled platter or individual plates lined with dressed lettuce. 8 servings.

BASIC WINE CHOICE: Fruity rosé

We sampled widely to find a mate for this softest and sweetest of salads, and always the choice came back to the softest and sweetest of rosés, pink Chablis; specifically, we enjoyed Gallo's. Widmer's Niagara falls in nicely here, too.

Cranberries in Wine Mold

This molded salad is designed particularly to go with turkey and avocado slices arranged on a platter.

1 medium orange
¾ cup dry white wine
1 package (3 ounces) lemon-flavored gelatin
1 can (1 pound) whole cranberry sauce

1 cup chopped pecans
Crisp lettuce leaves
About 1 cup commercial sour cream
Grated fresh orange peel

Force orange with peel through a food grinder fitted with a fine blade.

In a saucepan, combine the orange, with its juice, and wine; heat to boiling and boil for 1 minute. Remove from heat; add gelatin, and stir until dissolved. Stir in cranberry sauce and pecans. Turn into a 1-quart mold, or 6 individual molds. Chill until set.

Unmold onto a chilled platter or individual plates lined with lettuce. Sprinkle the sour cream with orange peel, and pass as a dressing. 6 servings.

174

BASIC WINE CHOICE: Sparkling wine

A wine that will get along with this tart assemblage of fruit must share with oranges their distinctive blend of sweet and sharp. Hanns Kornell's Extra Dry Champagne is a good first choice. If champagne seems extravagant, a Johannisberg Riesling is an agreeable substitute.

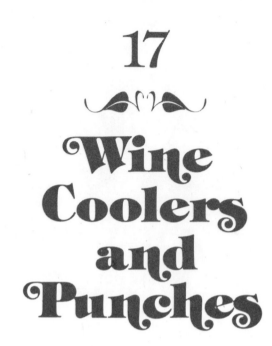

17

Wine Coolers and Punches

In addition to being good in its own right, wine is a great basic ingredient for refreshing punches in summer and soul-warming ones in winter.

Fresh flavors are the essence of summery punches; rich flavors belong at the heart of winter drinks. Neither kind of punch calls for expensive wine. The differences between fine wine and well-made but inexpensive wine are so subtle that any punch covers them up completely. It is a waste of both money and a subtle wine to use anything other than good jug wine in one of these punches. For the sparkling wine punches, seek out inexpensive bottles that say "Charmat" or "bulk process" on the label.

Champagne Orange Juice
178

Andaluza
178

Dry Vermouth on the Rocks with a Twist
178

Spritzer
179

Rosy Champagne Punch
179

Earl's Hot-Weather Concord Punch
179

Sherry Shrub
180

Cynthia's Red Flannel
180

Champagne Orange Juice

This drink is one of the best possible beginnings for a festive breakfast or brunch. The foods of breakfast follow it beautifully. If the meal is designed to continue with wine, you can keep sipping this or switch to champagne only or to a light and fruity white wine.
Sometimes this is called Mimosa, sometimes Champagne Continental.

1 part orange juice   **1 part chilled champagne**

For *each* serving, put 2 ice cubes in a large wine glass. Fill glass halfway with orange juice and then fill rest of glass with champagne.

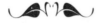

Andaluza

Combine orange juice and sherry for a slightly headier taste than Champagne Orange Juice. Appropriate for a little later in the day, Andaluzas make a good prelude to lunch and supper, too. Sherry and orange juice are Spanish flavors singly and together, so Spanish-type appetizers taste right—toasted almonds, pimiento-stuffed olives, ripe olives, shrimp, and thinly sliced, deeply smoked ham.
For a fresher effect, substitute dry vermouth for the sherry.

1 part orange juice   **1 part dry sherry**

Combine equal amounts of orange juice and sherry in a pitcher, and chill well. Stir, and pour into chilled wine glasses, or pour over ice cubes in large wine glasses.

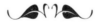

Dry Vermouth on the Rocks with a Twist

This is one of the best luncheon apéritifs.

Dry vermouth   **Fresh lemon peel**

For *each* serving, put 2 or 3 ice cubes into a large wine glass or old-fashioned glass. Pour dry vermouth over ice, and add a twist of fresh lemon peel.

Spritzer

A Spritzer is simply dry white wine with club soda added to lighten and brighten it. Of northern European ancestry, it is wonderful simply as a refreshing beverage for any time of the day—before or between meals, usually not with a meal.

You can substitute a dry rosé or red wine for the white, and you can change wine-to-soda proportions to please your taste.

1 part dry white wine   **1 part club soda**

For *each* serving, put ice cubes into a tall glass. Fill half the glass with wine, and fill rest of glass with soda. Stir very gently.

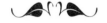

Rosy Champagne Punch

This is delicate and light in effect and color.

¼ cup sugar   **1 fifth bottle (4/5 quart)**
2 lemons, thinly sliced   **chilled pink champagne**

In a large pitcher or punch bowl, stir sugar with ¼ cup water until dissolved. Stir in lemon slices and chill for 1 hour. Add champagne and barely stir. Serve in wine glasses or punch cups—over ice cubes, if you wish. 8 servings.

Earl's Hot-Weather Concord Punch

You could hardly find an easier-to-make punch than this or one as good for a casual, hot day's refreshment. It is mild enough so that people can sip generously and intriguing enough to make them want seconds. We got the recipe from the artist Earl Thollander, who often serves it to guests around his sunny swimming pool. A dedicated home wine maker, Earl makes the punch with his own dry Concord grape wine. However, most commercial wines labeled "Concord" are too sweet for this recipe; closer approximations to Earl's homemade wine include the New York State Burgundies, Taylor's Lake Country Red, and their like.

The recipe is open to variation. You can use grapefruit soda instead of the orange, and you can increase or decrease the wine-to-soda proportions according to your taste.

1 part chilled dry   **1 part chilled orange soda**
**   native-grape red wine**

Pour equal parts of red wine and orange soda into a large pitcher or punch bowl or tall glasses over ice. Gently stir.

Sherry Shrub

Sherry Shrub is quite an old recipe. These days we streamline the making of it by using frozen lemonade concentrate.

It is important to chill the mixture for a good length of time before serving in order to let the flavors blend. Some say that the longer you chill it (up to about a month), the better it gets.

If you wish, you can add a splash of soda to each glass when serving.

1 fifth bottle (4/5 quart) dry sherry
1 can (6 ounces) frozen lemonade concentrate, undiluted

Juice of 2 fresh lemons

Shake or beat all ingredients together to mix thoroughly. Cover and refrigerate for 1 to 4 days or longer.

For *each* serving, pour about ½ cup of the mixture over ice cubes in a large wine glass. 10 servings.

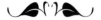

180

Cynthia's Red Flannel

Among the many, many manifestations of hot mulled wine, *glögg, gluh wein,* and all the other hot spiced red wines, we have found this to be a durable favorite. Its origins are Swedish.

You can cut back on the amount of vodka, if you wish. Or you can substitute brandy for the vodka. Cynthia says that her Red Flannel is "pretty boozy" when it is first made, but that it mellows after you have kept it at stay-hot temperature during the first round of drinks.

2 cups sugar
1 lemon, thinly sliced
1 cinnamon stick
1 tablespoon whole cloves
Seeds from 6 cardamom pods, crushed

1 cup seedless raisins, dark or golden
½ gallon dry red wine
1 quart vodka
Whole blanched almonds

In a large kettle, combine 4 cups water, sugar, lemon, cinnamon, cloves, cardamom, and raisins. Heat to boiling, remove from heat, and allow to cool. Add wine and vodka, and heat to serving temperature; do not boil.

Before serving, put an almond in the bottom of each cup; fill cups with hot beverage. 16 six-ounce servings.

Index